Keeping it Real

From the ready-made to the everyday
The D. Daskalopoulos Collection

Edited by Achim Borchardt-Hume

Artists represented in the D. Daskalopoulos Collection, Athens

Marina Abramović
Vito Acconci
Franz Ackermann
Haluk Akakçe
Alexis Akrithakis
Ana Laura Aláez
Ghada Amer
Carl Andre
Kostas Archaniotis
Kutluğ Ataman
Tonico Lemos Auad
Dimitris Baboulis
John Baldessari
Matthew Barney
Lynda Benglis
Joseph Beuys
Ashley Bickerton
Marc Bijl
Karla Black
John Bock
Louise Bourgeois
Mark Bradford
Christoph Büchel
Chris Burden
Helen Chadwick
Paul Chan
Jake & Dinos Chapman
Nikos Charalambidis
Christos Charissis
Savvas Christodoulides
Dan Colen
George Condo
Abraham Cruzvillegas
José Damasceno
Wim Delvoye
José Antonio Hernández Díez
Christina Dimitriadis
Mark Dion
Marcel Duchamp
Sam Durant
Jimmie Durham
Dora Economou
Inka Essenhigh
Peter Fischli & David Weiss
Michel François
Tom Friedman
Kendell Geers
Gelitin
Gilbert & George
Robert Gober
Antony Gormley
Subodh Gupta
Guyton\Walker
David Hammons
Keith Haring
Rachel Harrison
Mona Hatoum
Arturo Herrera
Thomas Hirschhorn
Damien Hirst
Jim Hodges
Evan Holloway
Jenny Holzer
Rebecca Horn
Pierre Huyghe
Kostas Ioannidis
Despina Isaia
Christian Jankowski
Isaac Julien
Konstantin Kakanias
Vlassis Kaniaris
Anastasia Karvela
Mike Kelley
William Kentridge
Nikos Kessanlis
Martin Kippenberger
Jeff Koons
Sophia Kosmaoglou
Joseph Kosuth
Jannis Kounellis
Bose Krishnamachari
Barbara Kruger
Gabriel Kuri
Sia Kyriakakou
George Lappas
Sherrie Levine
Justin Lieberman
Stathis Logothetis
Maria Loizidou
Michelle Lopez
Nate Lowman
Sarah Lucas
Ana Mathiou
Paul McCarthy
Steve McQueen
Julie Mehretu
Annette Messager
Antonis Michailidis
Maro Michalakakos
Aernout Mik
Tracey Moffatt
Robert Morris
Frini Mouzakitou
Wangechi Mutu
Bruce Nauman
Nikos Navridis
Ernesto Neto
Rivane Neuenschwander
Kori Newkirk
Tim Noble & Sue Webster
Cady Noland
Chris Ofili
Jan Van Oost
Gabriel Orozco
Tony Oursler
Aliki Palaska
Angelos Papadimitriou
Cornelia Parker
Anna Parkina
Ester Partegàs
Tassos Pavlopoulos
Paul Pfeiffer
Seth Price
Jannis Psychopedis
Alexandros Psychoulis
Marc Quinn
Walid Raad\The Atlas Group
Rashid Rana
Tobias Rehberger
Pipilotti Rist
Ry Rocklen
Tracey Rose
Julian Rosefeldt
Dieter Roth
Georgia Sagri
Doris Salcedo
Charles Sandison
Beverly Semmes
Kiki Seror
Andres Serrano
Jim Shaw
Cindy Sherman
Andreas Slominski
Kiki Smith
Josh Smith
Marios Spiliopoulos
Haim Steinbach
Jessica Stockholder
Daniel Subkoff
Do-Ho Suh
Takis
Paul Thek
Rosemarie Trockel
Stefanos Tsivopoulos
Costas Tsoclis
Dimitris Tsoublekas
Nobuko Tsuchiya
Keith Tyson
Meyer Vaisman
Dimitra Vamiali
Catharina Van Eetvelde
Adriana Varejão
Costas Varotsos
Bill Viola
Andreas Vousouras
Kelley Walker
Mark Wallinger
Andy Warhol
Rebecca Warren
Gary Webb
Eric Wesley
Franz West
Rachel Whiteread
Sue Williams
Christopher Wool
Iskender Yediler

Art is but a vision of reality

W. B. Yeats, 'Ego Dominus Tuus' (1917)

Contents

Forewords 06

Prologue 10
Act 1: The Corporeal 16
Act 2: Subversive Abstraction 52
Act 3: Current Disturbance 80
Act 4: Material Intelligence 92
List of works 122

Further reading 125
Image credits 126
Index 128
Acknowledgements 130

Sponsor's foreword

It is a pleasure to support the Whitechapel Gallery's inspiring initiative of presenting collections as part of its diverse programme. This collaboration with a collector of such stature as Dimitris Daskalopoulos reinforces the Whitechapel Gallery's international reputation as a dynamic public gallery leading in its field. Under Achim Borchardt-Hume's intelligent curatorship, we look forward to a year-long exhibition which will sample the D. Daskalopoulos Collection by way of four thematic displays. From Marcel Duchamp to Martin Kippenberger and Robert Gober, we will have the opportunity for a serious review of some of the 20th and 21st centuries' most original artists.

The Whitechapel's dedicated Collections Gallery is proving a resounding success as is apparent from the overwhelmingly positive response to the earlier displays of works from the British Council Collection curated by guest artists and art historians. We are delighted that these will now be followed by a European collection of such significance.

Robert Hiscox, Chairman, Hiscox Insurance

Dimitris Daskalopoulos's foreword

Art is both a subjective and collective endeavour which derives from and is, at the same time, proof of the human gift for creativity. It appears an utterly natural and self-evident – yet also strangely enigmatic – metaphor for our shared existence. Art and the ability to consciously create something that did not exist before are, to me, the key features that distinguish us humans from other species. I attribute this inventive imperative to the same essential and urgent 'creative impulse' that drives all human action, as mysterious as it is real.

Through my collection I seek to identify and to bring together depictions of this reality, this mystery, this essence as I see them expressed in artists' works. By putting different works of art in dialogue with one another, I attempt to find an analogy for the constant tension between life and death, between our desire for immortality and the futility of many of our daily struggles, an expression of what it means to be human with all its challenges. No matter how difficult the subjects art may be dealing with, in the end it inherently testifies to our propensity towards optimism and improvement rather than nihilism and abandon.

I am truly delighted that the collection is having its first public presentation within the context of an institution as prestigious as the Whitechapel Gallery: an institution world-renowned for its history of innovation and being in the very vanguard of artistic development.

It has been a welcome opportunity to be exposed to an erudite reading and critique of the collection. I have marvelled at the creative process of curating this year-long exhibition and the attention lavished on shaping each of the four individual displays. A private collection is a pre-existing repository of works accumulated over a long period of time. In a sense it is already 'curated' in that it is the result of a continuous, and often very personal, process of adding works while excluding others. During the many conversations around *Keeping it Real*, I saw the intricacies of this process revisited, new interpretations articulated of works I felt were old friends, and eye-opening connections being made between works that made me see them in a new light.

I hope that this innovative model for a collaboration between a public institution and a private collection as pioneered by the Whitechapel Gallery and the D. Daskalopoulos Collection to bring art in private hands to a wide public will flourish long into the future.

After all, bringing inspiration and excitement to this public by way of showing thought-provoking, surprising and at times challenging works of art is a goal we wholeheartedly share.

Dimitris Daskalopoulos

Director's foreword

An art collector might be defined as an individual with a passion for aesthetics and the resources to satisfy their desire. The truly great art collectors are also risk takers. The museum curator must be cautious about acquisitions, acceding to the endorsement of history and the collective acceptance of critics, colleagues, funders and boards. By contrast collectors can trust intuition and take a gamble on buying an unknown artist or a provocative work of art, simply because it speaks to them and to their times.

The Whitechapel Gallery is a kunsthalle and does not own a collection. But it has shown collections since its founding in 1901, using the bodies of works assembled by individuals or institutions, to introduce local audiences to art from around the world. Over a century these collections have provided an insight into Chinese, Indian, Japanese and Middle Eastern art; and given access to the great movements of Western art.

Keeping it Real celebrates a 21st century collection brought together by one collector. It exemplifies courage in acquiring emerging artists; and commitment in embracing challenging works. It is also a collection that brings to its own locale – Athens – canonical modern artists that are not represented in Greece but are of great historical significance.

This book and the exhibition it accompanies are conceived, like a theatre play, in four acts. Unfolding over the course of a year each of the four displays 'performs' one aspect of an overarching narrative. Through the selection of more than fifty works from the D. Daskalopoulos Collection the exhibition examines a particular engagement with materiality in recent art that can be traced back to Marcel Duchamp's revolutionary gesture of the ready-made. Works by household names are shown alongside those by artists rarely seen in London or exhibiting at the Whitechapel Gallery for the first time.

The remarkable spectrum of modern and contemporary art brought together in this collection also enables an exploration of specific themes that have characterised the art of our times, which interrelate and speak to each other through the four acts.

We are indebted to the generosity of Mr. and Mrs. D. Daskalopoulos for allowing the Whitechapel Gallery unrestricted access to their collection and for sharing a substantial part of it with our audiences over the course of one year. We also thank François Chantala, Thomas Dane, Dimitris Paleocrassas, Calum Sutton and Ioanna Vryzaki for their enthusiastic support of this project and their help with countless logistical questions. On behalf of our Trustees I would like to express our gratitude to the staff of the Gallery, in particular Achim Borchardt-Hume, Chief Curator for his curatorial vision and insightful essay; and Shamita Sharmacharja, Exhibition Organiser for her contribution in the production of the displays and the publication. Our thanks also go to Simon Elliott and Gary Martyniak of Rose Design for their elegant and sensitive book design and to all the artists, individuals and institutions who have kindly agreed to their works being reproduced in this context. Finally, we are deeply grateful to Robert Hiscox and Elliot MacDonald of Hiscox for their vital support in giving important collections a public platform.

Iwona Blazwick, OBE, Director

Prologue

Prologue

When my little girl falls on the pavement and her teeth go through her lower lip and I have to take her to the hospital and watch her get stitches, I don't really think about 'almost real'. I don't think about what's real anymore.
Richard Prince[1]

In 1917, soon after his arrival in New York, Marcel Duchamp, under the pseudonym R. Mutt, submitted a standard urinal for display at the annual exhibition of the American Society of Independent Artists. Although Duchamp was part of the Organising Committee and the Society had committed itself to showing every entry, *Fountain*, as Duchamp had satirically titled the urinal, was excluded on the grounds that it lacked artistic originality. Ironically, what would become one of the most influential works of twentieth-century art was known for more than forty years only from a black-and-white photograph by Duchamp's friend, Alfred Stieglitz. It was not until 1964 that Duchamp authorised an edition of *Fountain*, at which point it was no longer a mass-produced porcelain urinal that went on display, but a meticulously hand-crafted ceramic copy thereof.

The conflict between the literal qualities of artistic materials and their transcendence – or material and form – has been a constant since the early days of Modernism. One has only to think of the use of newspaper in Cubist collage or the way found objects were incorporated into Constructivist and Dadaist compositions. Duchamp had first begun to experiment with his so-called ready-mades, everyday objects turned into art, in 1913 in his Paris studio when he had combined a wooden stool and a single bicycle wheel into an absurd assemblage. Shifting the focus of artistic intervention from a skill-based craft to the cerebral process of selection, he mobilised the tropes of institutional display such as plinth and title to challenge the limits of what could constitute art. Duchamp himself was always keen to emphasise the transformative potential of this gesture, rather than its anti-aesthetic implications: 'My *Fountain* was a not a negation: I simply tried to create a new idea for an object that everybody thought they knew. Anything can become something else, that is what I wanted to show.'[2]

Nonetheless, Duchamp's name over the years became synonymous with an attitude in art that eschewed materiality and physicality in favour of concept and idea. The art historian, Hal Foster, described the Frenchman's formative influence on a whole generation of artists throughout the late 1950s and 1960s thus: 'one sign of our difference (for our predecessors, no doubt, of our decadence) is that the angel with whom we wrestled was Marcel Duchamp by way of Andy Warhol, more than Picasso by way of Pollock.'[3] These artists' preoccupation with de-materialising the art object went so far as to cause Lawrence Weiner to declare that the work was only a proposition, and that it was of no relevance whether or not this was physically executed.

It may seem paradoxical therefore that in the 1980s, following the dissolution of medium-specificity, a great many artists who showed a renewed interest in the notion of the object, especially sculpture and installation, also cited Duchamp and the ready-made as their principal historic reference points; all the more so, as these artists also paid attention to the process of making in a manner not seen for some time before. Where the studio had traditionally been a place for solitary contemplation it now became a workshop, with artists directing the best technicians available to achieve the desired result, leaving no material out of bounds for the production of their work. 'Making', Alain Cueff observed in his study of 1980s art, 'remains a way of simultaneously testing both the material and its possible forms, and as such both its immediate results and long-term consequences are unpredictable.'[4]

The interest in non-traditional art materials shared by many of these artists was motivated not least by their ambition to establish a more immediate nexus between their work and the social, cultural and political contexts they found themselves operating in. This was especially true at the beginning of the decade when, following forty years of localised peace in the West, the spreading AIDS epidemic acted as a stark reminder of human vulnerability. In his seminal study of the period, Hal Foster aptly identified its prevalent mood as *The Return of the Real.*[5]

Works by artists such as Louise Bourgeois, Robert Gober, David Hammons, Mike Kelley and Kiki Smith, who were central to this moment, form the backbone of the D. Daskalopoulos Collection. They also act as a starting point for this series of four micro-exhibitions. *Keeping it Real* is conceived as one exhibition unfolding in four acts, with each one loosely responding to what goes before. Central to all is the way in which works by a diverse range of artists from the past fifty or so years recruit their meaning from the materials deployed. This persistent engagement with materiality, often motivated by very different agendas, is traced here via correspondences – formal, conceptual and visual – detected among 53 from the more than 400 works in the collection.

Act 1: The Corporeal focuses on the body as the biological arena in which identity is formed. This notion was central to the re-emergence of a new realism in the 1980s and has retained a currency with artists exploring questions of mortality, gender, sexuality and ethnicity to this day. *Act 2: Subversive Abstraction* examines the innovative ways in which the formal language of abstraction and the material conventions of painting from the 1960s onwards were used to narrow the gap between the autonomous art object and the world at large. The lack of clearly discernible subject matter stands in sharp contrast to the prevalence of the human form in the first act. *Act 3: Current Disturbance* displays a single large-scale installation by Mona Hatoum of the same title. Combining references to both the body and abstraction, *Current Disturbance* is shown here for the first time in London, an important testament to the D. Daskalopoulos Collection's commitment to preserving ambitious installation works. The final act, *Material Intelligence*, focuses on the work of artists who engage with the everyday, including image and reproduction, as yet another type of material. Rather than mourn the failure of the modernist utopia, these artists search its legacy for ideas that may still prove fertile for the future.

Keeping it Real is but one approach to displaying a selection of works from one of the most significant European collections of recent art in private hands. However, it seems a pertinent one as it starts not with the person of the collector – though the four micro-exhibitions give a concise, but representative glimpse of the unique character of his collection – but with the centrality of the work of art. Tracing a particular sensibility and material engagement in a diverse range of works, *Keeping it Real* shows that art, rather than seeking an escape route from reality, offers a much needed space for critical reflection to grapple with the pressing issues of our time. In an age anxious to understand what still constitutes authentic experience, *Keeping it Real* reminds us that art does not exist outside this world, or what is commonly called reality, but is a vital part of it.

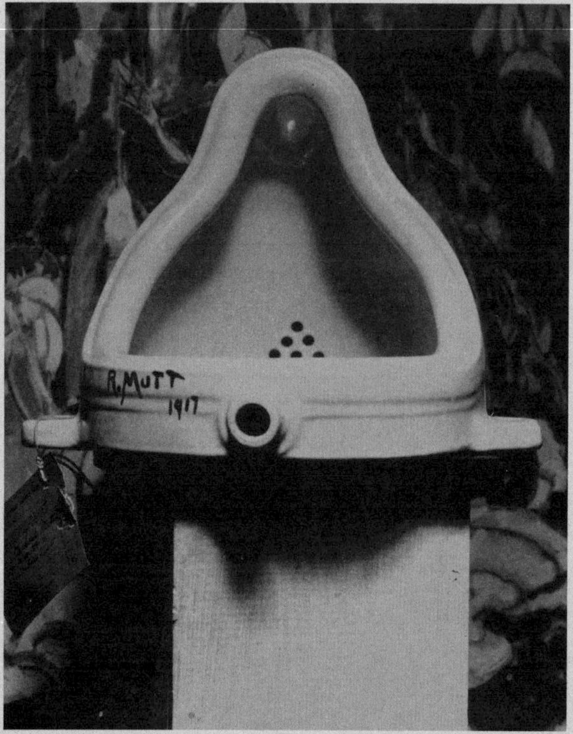

Alfred Stieglitz
Fountain, photograph of sculpture by Marcel Duchamp
(1917)
Gelatin silver print
23.5 x 17.7 cm

Notes

1. Richard Prince in interview with Steve Lafreniere, *Artforum*, (March 2003), 71.
2. Marcel Duchamp, in conversation with Ulf Linde (1961), cited in Harald Szeeman, ed., *Marcel Duchamp* (Basel and Ostfildern-Ruit: Museum Jean Tinguely Basel and Hatje Cantz: 2002) 90.
3. Hal Foster, *The Return of the Real* (Cambridge and London: October/ MIT Press, 1996)
4. Alain Cueff, 'The Artwork – The Work', in Ulrich Loock, ed., *The 80s. A Typology* (Porto; Museu Serralves: 2007) 45.
5. Hal Foster, op. cit.

The Corporeal Act

1

The Corporeal

I like transgressional boundaries, leaky distinctions, dualisms, fractured identities, monstrosity and perversity. I like contamination. I like miscegenation. I like a fly in the soup, a pie in the face. I like the territory of slapstick, where amidst general laughter neither death nor crime exists. I like the world of burlesque with its pure gesticularity. In this guiltless world, where everyone gives and receives blows at will, buildings fall down, bricks fly, the protagonists are immortal and violence is universal, without consequence.
Sherrie Levine[1]

The human body is one of the most common and readily available subjects in the history of Western art. Idealised, it was especially the female body that was offered as erotic object to the male gaze, a gender hierarchy that continued to pervade the historic avant-gardes, from Cubism to Surrealism. Throughout the mid-twentieth century the body became increasingly sublimated. American post-war painting, in particular, replaced its representation with the use of scale to establish a physical rapport between canvas and viewer. Out of this grew Minimalism's pre-occupation with the relationship between the object, the space it inhabits and the phenomenological experience this generates. Soon after, Conceptual art took the idea of de-materialising the art object even further by making text and language its privileged form of expression.

It was not until the latter part of the twentieth century that the body made a renewed appearance, initially in a very direct way, in happenings and performances; and soon after in sculptures and installations which, in the words of Hal Foster, pushed illusionism 'to the point of the real, not to cover up the real with simulacral surfaces... but to uncover it in uncanny things.'[2] Many of these works share a previously unseen physical directness to address the viewer. Especially in the US, a growing number of artists, who were keenly invested in the feminist debate, gay rights and freedom movements, began to explore the body as a site of conflict between personal needs and social expectations. Fragile, vulnerable and often fragmented, the body was revealed as being susceptible to drives and desires beyond the power of sublimation, with psychological and physical trauma a constant risk. Themes such as gender, sexuality and ethnicity were foregrounded to expose the limitations of the white, male, heterosexual perspective which had hitherto dominated much of the social and artistic discourse. The aesthetic strategies employed by these artists, their use of materials and emphatic assertion of the autonomous objecthood of the work of art was historically rooted in Marcel Duchamp's paradigmatic ready-made which imported signifiers of everyday life into the realm of art to imbue them with an altogether different meaning.

Fountain (1917/1964), a urinal displayed lying flat on its backside, is perhaps Duchamp's most notorious ready-made. Many of Duchamp's works entail playful allusions to the human body and its drives and desires. However, few of his works do so as overtly as *Fountain*, its scatological humour remaining key to its continuing provocative prowess. By applying to a standard urinal the tropes of display and institutional framing generally reserved for objects commonly recognised as works of art, Duchamp broke with centuries of the tradition of art as intellectually and morally elevating. The object itself has been deprived of its use value, not only by severing it from any plumbing and placing it on a plinth in a gallery, but, importantly, by turning it 90 degrees onto its back in the process. *Fountain* thus contests the importance of verticality to the hu(man)ist view of the world.[3]

Fountain also challenges the concept of universalism insofar as it is a clearly gendered object, familiar on a day-to-day basis to one half of the population only. Duchamp had tested gender stereotypes before via the creation of his female alter ego Rrose Sélavy. His play with gender transgression and dysfunction can be seen as much as an attack on the bourgeois values of art as on a patriarchal world view, especially if one bears in mind that *Fountain* was conceived at the time that World War I, the first fully industrialised war, was raging across Europe.

Assumptions about gender identity conditioned by a heterosexual world view and the role these play in the socialisation of the individual are also central cues to the work of Robert Gober, who first came to prominence in the 1980s at the height of the AIDS epidemic. Catholic by upbringing and openly gay, Gober has explored the many stereotypes that traditionally constrict homo- (and thereby hetero) sexual men.

A Pair of Basinless Sinks (1986) make direct reference to Duchamp's *Fountain* (Gober himself produced a series of wall-mounted urinals in 1988) and other 'plumbing-related' works by the Frenchman such as his *Drain Stopper* (1964), all of which play on the idea of receptacles unable to receive. *Fountain*'s dysfunction is mirrored by the sinks' missing basins as all we get to see are the wall-mounted splash-backs. In their austerity they are not unlike gravestones, emblematic perhaps of the climate of fear and grief that characterised 1980s New York during the AIDS epidemic, a time the artist recalls as when death temporarily overtook life in the city.[4]

Like many of Gober's works, the sinks are modelled on the domestic furniture of US housing in the 1950s and 1960s, a period of exceptional social conformity which Gober, who realised his own homosexuality early in his childhood, experienced as particularly repressive. In their inability to perform, the sinks are pervaded by an air of loss and melancholia, two notions that are central to Gober's work. The precise object of this loss though remains unclear.

This air of ambiguity is even more evident in *Untitled* (1991), a wax torso one half of which is characterised as predominantly male, the other as principally female. However, the boundaries are blurred as hairs from the male half invade the female side, and the male chest shows signs of softness. Gender belongs to the first level of identity ascribed to the body and according to Freudian thinking provides the basis for psycho-sexual development. Therefore, Gober appears to deduce that if gender is unclear, then so is sexuality; which begs the question who is the subject and who the object of desire?

The motive of the double-gendered torso first appeared in Gober's *Slides of a Changing Painting* (1982–83), a slide-projection which captures the multiple stages of a single painting that Gober repeatedly overlaid with new images. Years later, when he accidentally chanced on a reproduction of one of the slides, he decided to turn the image into a sculpture. The base form is cast from a 100-pound bag of plaster, a reference to Gober's earlier casts of cat litter bags. The wax can be read as both an allusion to Gober's Catholic heritage and the ephemeral nature of existence. Mute and passive, *Untitled* coalesces oppositional categories such as gender which are elemental for the construction of meaning to create an atmosphere of 'dangerous harmlessness' instead.[5]

Assumptions about authenticity and originality – as they underpin both the discourse around art and the formation of personal identity – are at the heart of Sherrie Levine's practice. *Fountain (Buddha): 5* (1996) is a direct riff on Duchamp's urinal.[6] However, where Duchamp displayed an industrial object Levine presents its highly polished bronze simulacrum. It should not be forgotten in this context that for decades the original *Fountain* was known from reproduction only, and that the edition made in the 1960s under Duchamp's supervision is in fact a meticulously hand-crafted copy rather than a mass-produced commodity.[7] Levine, in turn, cast her *Fountain (Buddha): 5* from a standard urinal produced by J. L. Mott Iron Works, the same company which had manufactured Duchamp's original. Importantly, she selected the urinal for her cast not by comparing it directly to Duchamp's *Fountain* but to a series of reproductions in a monograph she had picked up from a thrift shop.

Translating Duchamp's ready-made into polished bronze once more foregrounds the urinal's sculptural qualities: 'I thought it would be challenging to work in a traditional sculpture material – something with an immediate aesthetic credibility. I was very surprised when I saw my first *Fountain*. When I made the decision to cast the urinal, I was thinking primarily about Duchamp, but the finished high polish bronze sculpture more readily evoked Brancusi and Arp.'[8] Levine, of course, knew about the connection between Duchamp and Brancusi, and that the former had acted as the latter's US representative when

Robert Gober
Selection from *Slides of a Changing Painting* (1982–1983)
35mm slides
Collection Walker Art Center, Minneapolis

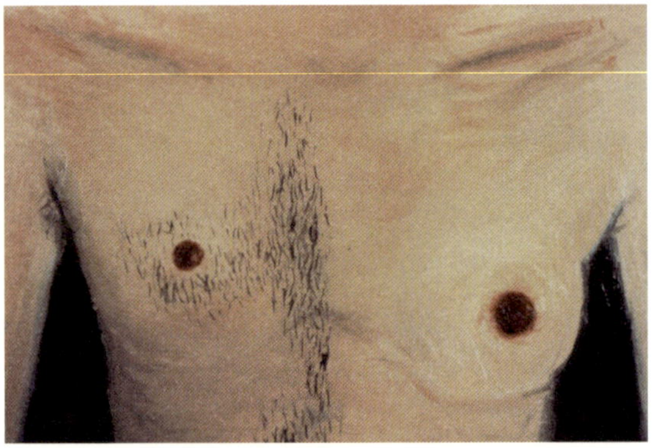

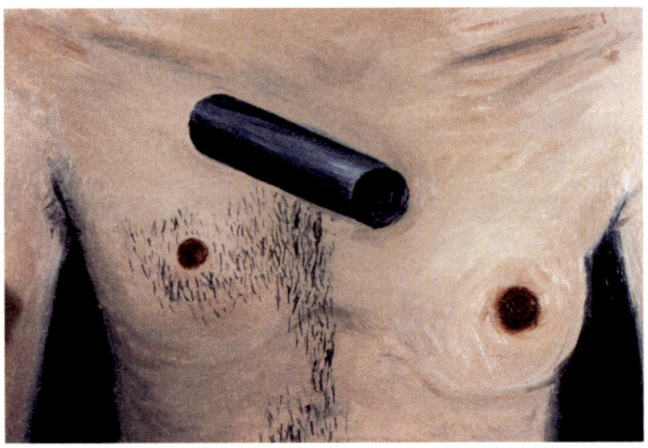

Brancusi's sculptures were denied the status of art works and classified as industrial design instead.[9] It is noteworthy in this context that the critical discourse around *Fountain* itself at first primarily appraised the formal beauty of the urinal as an industrial object, and that it was only during the 1950s and 1960s, as Duchamp was being rediscovered by a younger generation of artists, that the focus shifted to the anti-retinal implications of the ready-made. In 1996, in his biography of Duchamp, Calvin Tomkins once more applauded the sculptural qualities of *Fountain*, likening the urinal's flowing outline to that of a seated Buddha, which may account for the reference in Levine's title.[10]

Levine has applied similar strategies of doubling and translation to objects from completely different cultural realms. *Body Mask* (2007) is one of a series of bronze casts of a ritualistic wooden mask carried by young men belonging to the Makonde in south-eastern Tanzania during initiation rites to demarcate gender roles. By casting these masks and replacing their original context with that of a gallery environment, Levine queries numerous assumptions about gender and identity-formation. She also raises questions about artistic originality and whether it is actually possible to conceive any work without debt to something else that came before. Modernism's complex relationship with the so-called 'primitive' is expanded here to an interrogation of the fetishistic qualities with which divergent societies imbue their artefacts, be they ritualistic masks or works of art.

The Surrealist fascination with the found object and the uncanny loomed large in the 1980s which led to the re-discovery of artists such as Louise Bourgeois, who though active since the 1930s, had only recently come to wider public and critical attention. *Fillette (Sweet Version)* (1968–99) commands the atavistic awe of the fetish, its raw materiality and explicit sexuality transforming it into a disturbing counterpart to the cerebral coolness of Duchamp's *Fountain*. *Fillette* takes the form of an oversized male member, whose carefully crafted surface varies between areas of surprising smoothness and others suggestive of flayed skin. Much of the object's effect depends on its presentation. In a 1982 photograph by Robert Mapplethorpe, Bourgeois is seen cradling *Fillette* under her right arm while smiling mischievously at the camera. Her gesture appears protective rather than aggressive, directed at the young girl of the object's title. However, when hung vertically, the member appears threateningly erect and disarmingly castrated at the same time. Elsewhere, Bourgeois, wife and mother to three sons, has commented: 'I consider the masculine attributes to be extremely delicate; they're objects that the woman, thus myself, must protect.'[11] In its ambiguities of scale, surface and direction, *Fillette* becomes a highly unnerving object that touches on deep-rooted fears and anxieties.

When Paul Thek first exhibited his disturbing sculptures and dissonantly joyous paintings in the 1960s in New York, his art seemed somewhat out of kilter with the times. Always an outsider, Thek, who died of AIDS in 1988 aged 55, had strong spiritual leanings and a distrust of American values that eventually lead him to emigrate to Europe. While critically neglected for much of his lifetime, his work gained a wider currency in the 1980s in the context of other artists concerned with the politics of the body. Thek is especially known for his sculptures of meticulously crafted faux flesh such as *Meat Cable* (1969), whose visceral presence stands in marked contrast to the purity of the white cube gallery. Thek himself has commented: 'I was amused with the idea of meat [...] because I thought it made fun of the scene – where the name of the game seemed to be "how cool can you be" and "how refined". Nobody ever mentioned anything that seemed real. The world was falling apart. Anyone could see it. I was a wreck, the block was a wreck, the city was a wreck; and I'd go to a gallery and there would be a lot of fancy people looking at a lot of stuff that didn't say anything about anything to anyone.'[12]

Sue Williams also mobilises the uncanny, or what Freud originally called *unheimlich* – the unhomely – in her collages, albeit in a far more understated way. Williams is best known for her large-scale paintings that combine De-Kooning style colourful brushwork with cartoon-like animations of bodily

Robert Mapplethorpe
Louise Bourgeois (1982)
Gelatin silver print

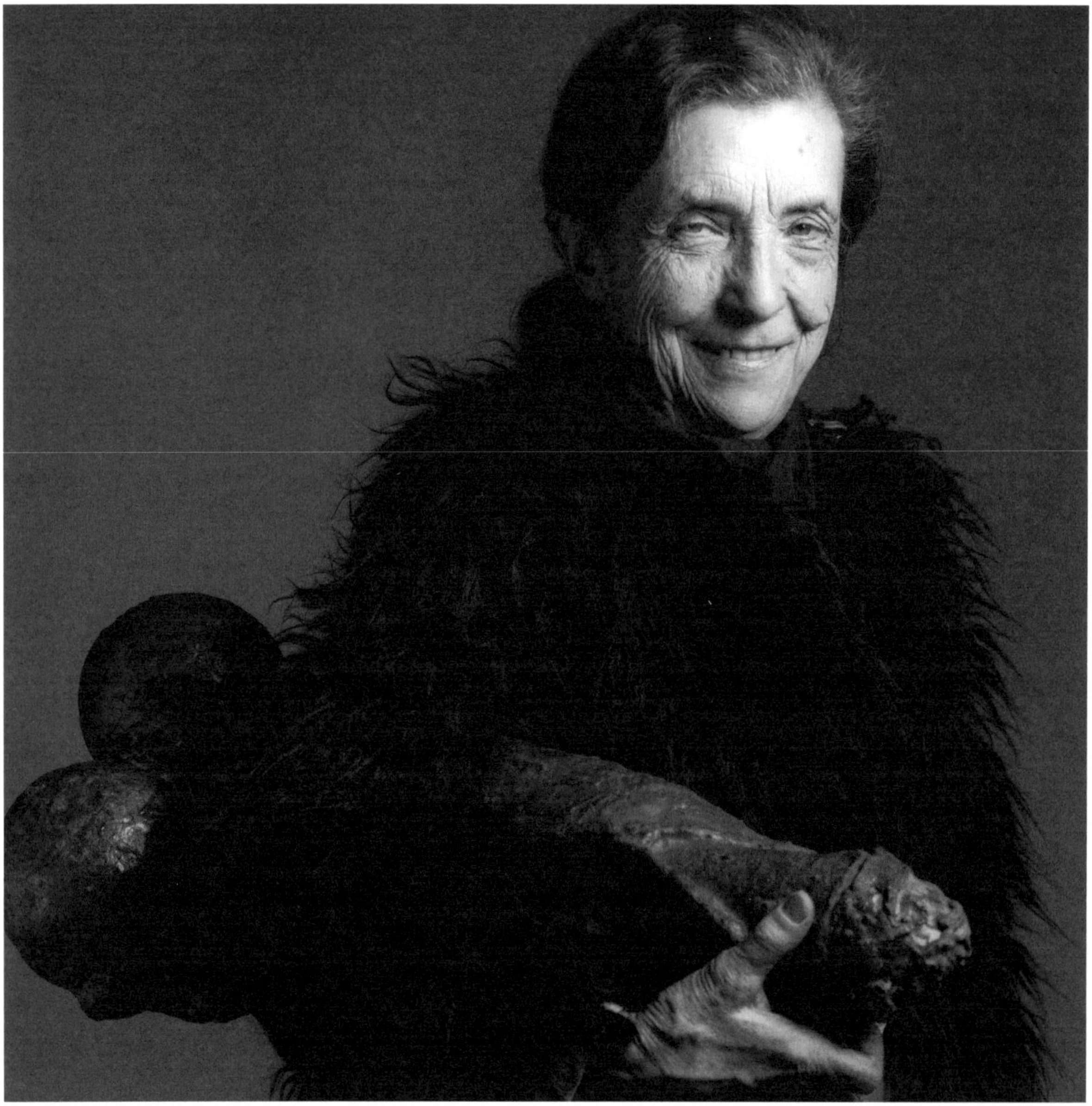

orifices, thus creating an ironic comment on modernist abstraction's attempt to sublimate all that is considered impure. In her collages she unites richly patterned wallpaper samples with doodlings depicting sex, a boy shamefully turning his back on the viewer, and cartoonish legs emerging from an amorphous body. Whereas the wallpaper suggests the cocooned safety of the family home, the drawings reveal the domestic sphere as being full of secrets; they are reminders of all that must be repressed if the illusions of innocence and respectability are to be maintained.

This debt to Surrealist strategies is also apparent in Sarah Lucas' *Bunny Gets Snookered* (1997). Everyday objects such as tights, cushion padding and a chair are assembled into a disturbing tableau of sexual offering, violence and mutilation. The use of tights to construct this headless pile of contorted limbs is highly fetishistic, the final result reminiscent of the Surrealist photographer Hans Bellmer's images of his bondaged doll. While the title with its allusions to pop culture and slang suggests that all of this is only a game, a bit of harmless fun, sex and death are linked here in a highly disconcerting way.

Performance was an important starting point for the re-introduction of the body into artistic practice. Marina Abramović was one of the first artists in the 1980s to re-engage with performance following the medium's earlier hey-day in the late 1960s and 1970s. *Cleaning the Mirror I* (1995) is one of three performances Abramović executed as part of a residency in Oxford. Performed directly for the camera with no audience present, Abramović can be seen vigorously scrubbing a dusty skeleton from the anthropological collection of the Pitt Rivers Museum. Her performance was inspired by Tibetan Buddhist rituals in which monks have to gain familiarity with death by dancing or sleeping with corpses so as to overcome the existential fear of the body when it encounters its nemesis. Image and audio were recorded simultaneously, the relentless sound of the brushing conveying the intensity of Abramović's action. The pathos of the film stands in sharp contrast with the material honesty of its presentation, with the dissection of the image reminiscent of the Surrealist game of the *cadavre exquis*. Death thus becomes as normal as it becomes grotesque.

The four light boxes in *Untitled* (1980) show the artist Kiki Smith washing her hands in blood. Smith is one of the most prominent artists of her generation continuously to investigate the visceral nature of the human body and how this is often subject to constraining social conventions. The daughter of the sculptor Tony Smith, she was familiar from an early age with the conventions of sculpture, helping her father with the construction of his geometric structures. Later, Smith literally turned these conventions inside out by using her own body as a mould for the making of sculptural shells such as in *Shitbody* (1992). The image was taken by Wojnarowicz, a gay rights activist, who was also an untrained painter, writer, film maker and performance artist. Aside from producing his own work, Wojnarowicz frequently collaborated with artists such as Smith or the photographer Nan Goldin. Smith's performance seems like an uncanny premonition of the AIDS virus which was first officially named in 1981 and which claimed millions of lives, including Wojnarowicz's.

Performance also occupies a central place in the more recent practice of John Bock. This frequently takes the form of lectures or films, the preparatory drawings and props for which are subsequently exhibited as part of often highly elaborate installations. *Winona Ryder* (2009) pays homage to one of the idols of Bock's youth. An image of the young actress features prominently in the wall hanging as do Bock's so-called *Meechbuildings*, little sculptures fashioned from everyday materials such as pizza and milk cartons, toilet rolls, ear cleaners and similar debris. *Meech* is the old German word for milk, an allusion to Bock's upbringing on a farm in rural Germany. The blue ground is covered with sausage-like tubes (made from socks) which regularly feature in Bock's films and performances. Here they are arranged to resemble a deliberately complex yet dysfunctional digestive system vaguely reminiscent of *The Honey Pump* which Bock's other idol, Joseph Beuys, exhibited at *Documenta* in 1977.

Having started as an activist in the American Indian movement, Jimmie Durham has observed of his working practice in the 1960s and 1970s: 'I was trying to make sense of something, I was trying to see if I could investigate certain things with objects, with doing things with materials.'[13] Though separated by four decades, a similar attitude to materiality still informs *No one will be harmed. This is only a test* (2008) which crosses the line between a ready-made and a relic of an actual event. The sculpture's main component, a metal-plated wooden board, shows the impact of various bullets fired by the artist as if for target practice. The placement at chest height invites the viewer to take a position of empathy with whoever had to seek shelter behind the board, it being unclear as to who the aggressor is, and who the victim. The strong performative quality of *No one will be harmed. This is only a test* with its implied threat of continued violence reminds the viewer of a communal sense of vulnerability, fears about which the tongue-in-cheek title at once assuages and reignites.

Taking ideas implicit in the ready-made and in performance one step further, various artists interested in issues of race, gender and sexuality draw on their own body for material. One of the earliest examples is David Hammons who, in the 1970s, developed a method of making prints by covering his body including his hair and clothes in margarine, pressing himself against a board, and then fixing the impression left by dusting it with chalk or pigment. Both the maker and the object of his work, Hammons introduced in a very immediate way the voice of African-Americans into a discourse from which it had hitherto been largely excluded. By their very nature the body prints play with the idea of positive and negative, a value association of which Hammons has observed: 'There's nothing negative about our images, it all depends on who's seeing it, and we've been depending on someone else's sight ... we have to look again and decide.'[14]

The spade is a recurring motif in Hammons' work of the period, both in body prints and sculptural objects. Rooted in a complex etymology, the word spade in slang is used as a derogatory and offensive term to label a black person. Hammons has made it a conscious strategy to appropriate signifiers frequently linked by way of negative connotations to clichés around black culture – such as the dreadlocks in *Untitled (Hair Piece)* (1975–76) or the imprints of a penis in *Blue Angels* (c.1970s) – to challenge whose voice is, and whose is not, being admitted to the pantheon of high art.

More recently, Jim Hodges has invented a highly original method of printing by using his own saliva as a medium. The delicate, spidery doodles of writing in *Untitled (Everything So Alive Lively Living)* (2006) were first drawn on a large sheet of paper which the artist then licked to moisten the drawing sufficiently for it to be transferred onto a second sheet. It is this trace of the original which is exhibited as the final work, the smudged ink mixed with saliva taking on the quality of a scientific sample in a Petri dish. The blue flowers are a tribute both to Romanticism and Jean Genet, whose writings hold an important place in Hodge's thinking. Avoiding over-determined references to gay politics, Hodge's poetic approach instead celebrates the generative potential of the creative act.

Debris of the artist's own body is also the material for Despina Isaia's *Untitled* (2003). Woven from the ponytail she cut off on the threshold to adulthood, it combines the artist's fascination with waste materials generated by the human body – including nails, hair and body peel – with her interest in transitional moments such as the one from girl to woman. The push-and-pull of attraction and repulsion, as it is inherent in the materiality of human hair depending on the context in which it is encountered, lends particular poignancy to the text, 'You are the beautiful reflection of his love's affection', a line from the 1968 musical *Funny Girl*. Many of Isaia's works deploy craft skills traditionally associated with female domestic duties, the shimmery sequins and romantic language standing in purposeful contrast to the act of cutting and the sense of loss this entails.

Notes

1. Catherine Ingraham, Sylvia Lavin and Howard Singerman, eds., *Sherrie Levine, Sculpture* (Cologne: Galerie Jablonka and Margo Leavin Gallery, 1996) n.p.
2. Hal Foster, *The Return of the Real* (Cambridge MA and London: October/MIT Press, 1996) 152.
3. Sigmund Freud in *Civilization and its Discontents* (1930) defined uprightness as central to the evolution of civilisation resulting in the privileging of the visual over the sense of smell, and the genital over the anal. Humanist art, with easel painting and erect sculpture its preferred mediums, also was emphatically upright. Lying on its back and utterly dysfunctional, Duchamp's *Fountain, avant-la-lettre* performed a full-frontal attack on the hierarchies onto which, according to Freud, Western culture is built.
4. Cited in Hal Foster, Rosalind Krauss, Yve-Alain Bois, Benjamin Buchloh, *Art Since 1900: Modernism, Antimodernism, Postmodernism* (London: Thames and Hudson, 2004) 646.
5. Theodora Vischer, *Robert Gober* (Basel: Museum für Gegenwartskunst, 1995) 42.
6. *Fountain* holds such importance for Levine and her complex construct of a historicity 'after' the event that it is the only work she has elaborated in two versions, one in 1991, the other in 1996, with the latter resembling Duchamp's original most closely.
7. For a detailed account of the material and critical history of *Fountain*, see also William A. Camfield, *Marcel Duchamp, Fountain* (Houston: The Menil Collection/Houston Fine Art Press, 1988).
8. Martha Buskirk, 'Interview with Sherrie Levine', Martha Buskirk and Mignon Nixon, eds., *The Duchamp Effect* (Cambridge MA and London: October/MIT Press, 1996) 179.
9. See also Daniel McClean and Armen Avanessian, 'Trials of the Title: The Trials of Brancusi and Veronese', in Daniel McClean, ed., *The Trials of Art* (London: Ridinghouse, 2007) 37–63. For a detailed analysis of the triangulation between Duchamp, Brancusi and Levine, see also Howard Singerman, 'Sherrie Levine's Shop Window Proof', in *Sherrie Levine, Sculpture*, op. cit., 9–18.
10. Calvin Tomkins, *Duchamp: A Biography* (New York: Henry Holt & Company, 1996) 186.
11. Cited in Frances Morris, ed., *Louise Bourgeois* (London: Tate, 2007) 146.
12. Cited in Richard Flood, 'Paul Thek: The Wonderful World That Almost Was', in R. Groenenboom, ed., *Paul Thek* (Barcelona: Fundació Antoni Tàpies, 1996) 212.
13. 'Dirk Snauwaert in conversation with Jimmie Durham' in Laura Mulvey, Dirk Snauwaert, Mark Alice Durant, eds., *Jimmie Durham* (London: Phaidon, 1995) 10.
14. Cited in Kellie Jones, 'The Structure of Myth and the Potency of Magic' in David Hammons, *David Hammons: Rousing the Rubble* (Cambridge MA & New York: MIT Press/ICA, 1991) 34.

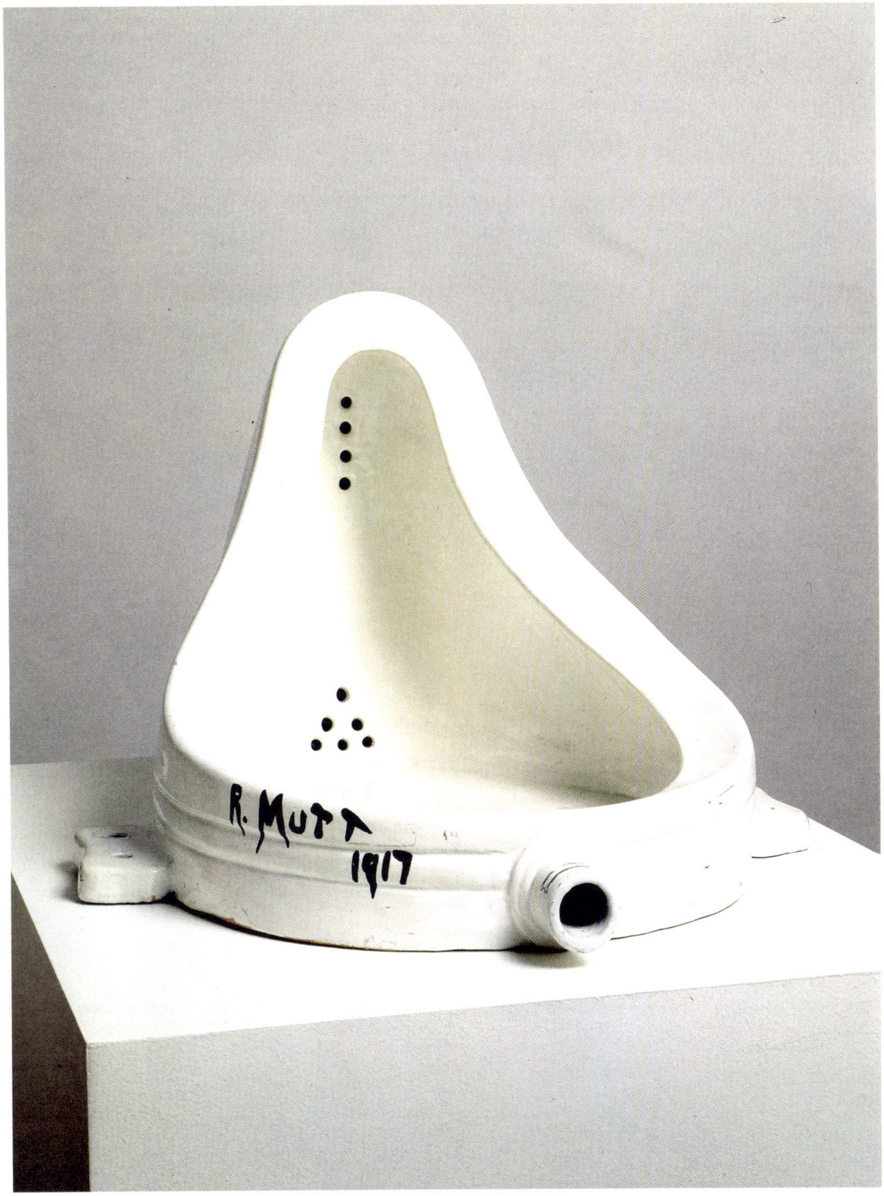

Marcel Duchamp
Fountain (1917/1964)
Glaze cast ceramic
urinal with black paint
35.6 x 49.1 x 62.6 cm

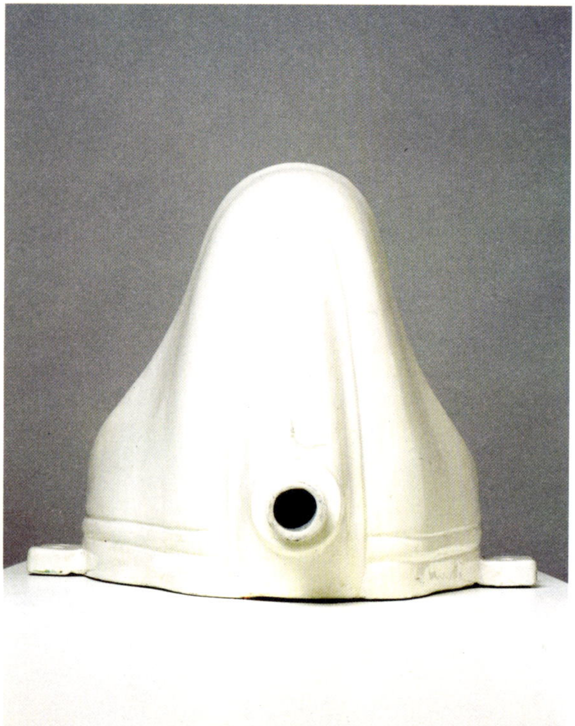

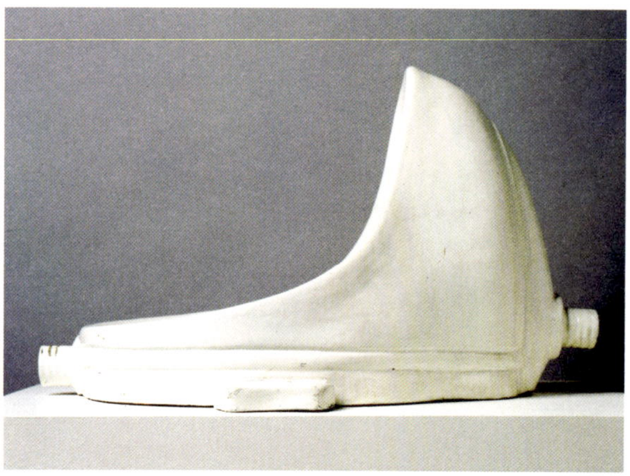

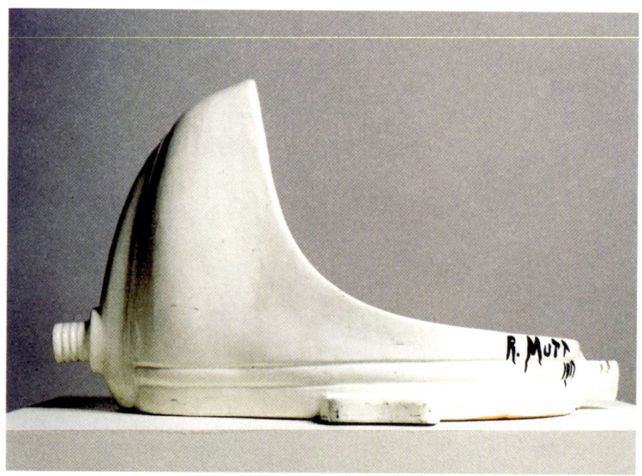

Marcel Duchamp
Fountain (1917/1964)
Glaze cast ceramic urinal
with black paint
35.6 x 49.1 x 62.6 cm

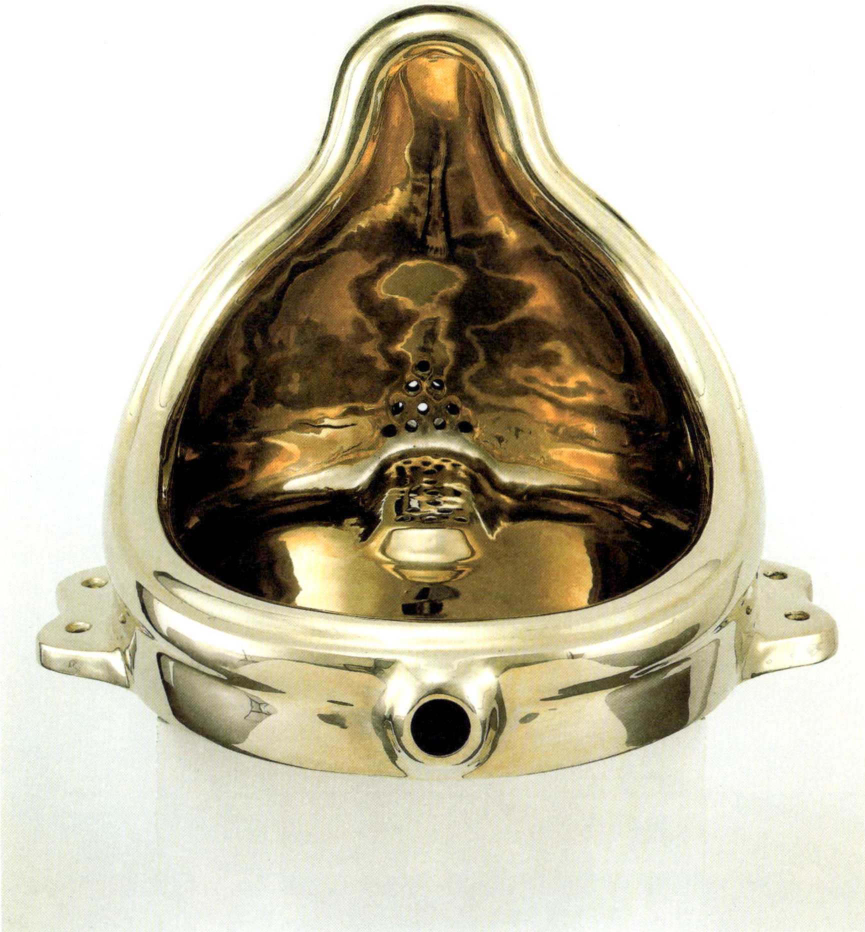

Sherrie Levine
Fountain (Buddha): 5 (1996)
Cast bronze
42.5 x 40 x 30 cm

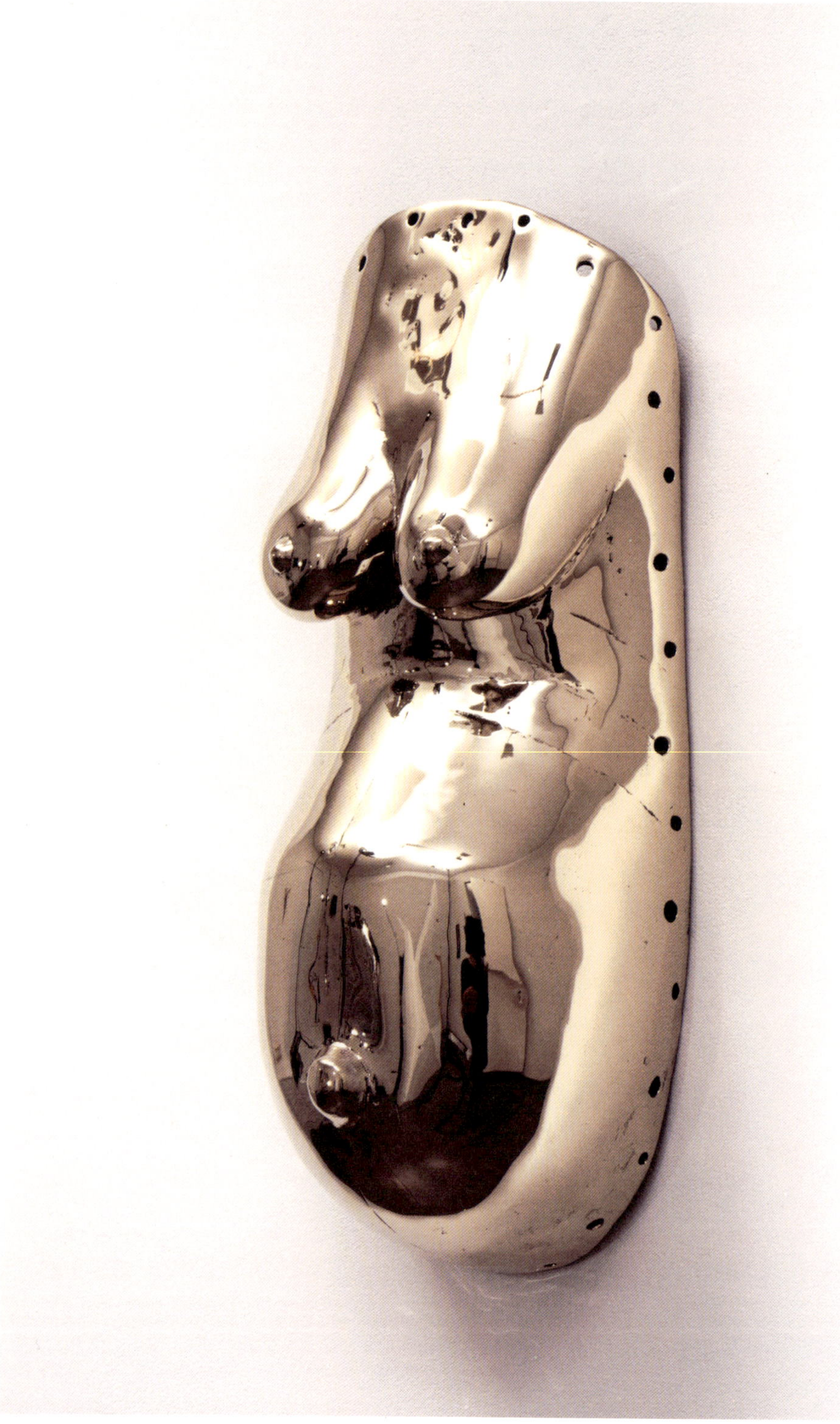

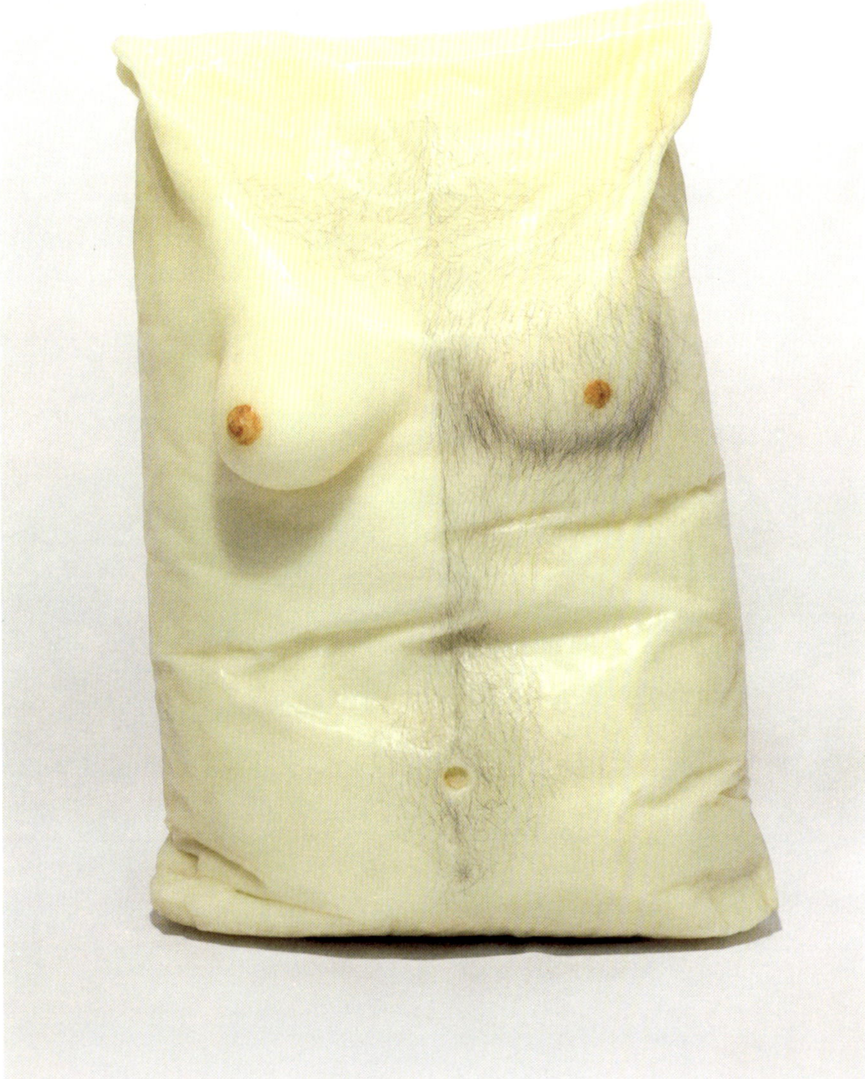

Sherrie Levine
Body Mask (2007)
Cast bronze
57.2 x 24.1 x 14.6 cm

Robert Gober
Untitled (1991)
Beeswax with hair, pigment
61 x 40 x 31 cm

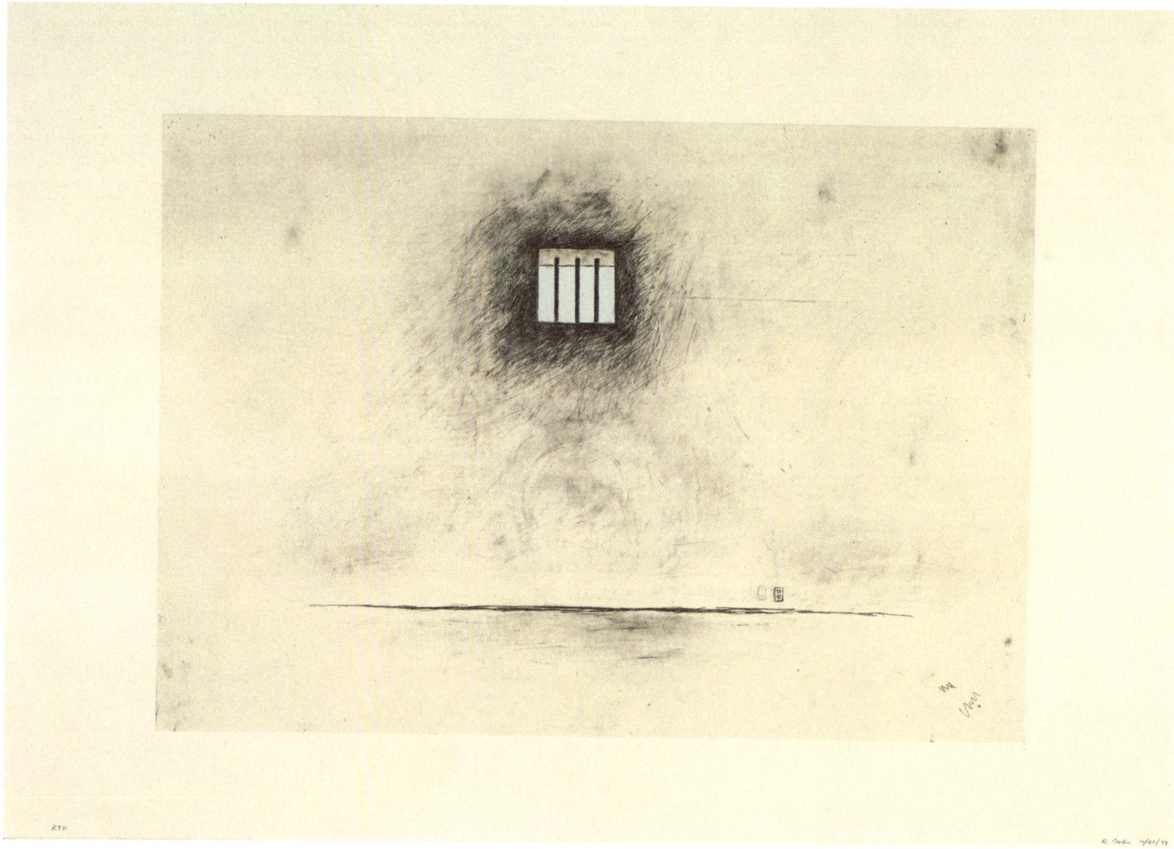

Robert Gober
Untitled (2000)
Lithograph, screen print,
mixed media on paper
55.9 x 81.3 cm

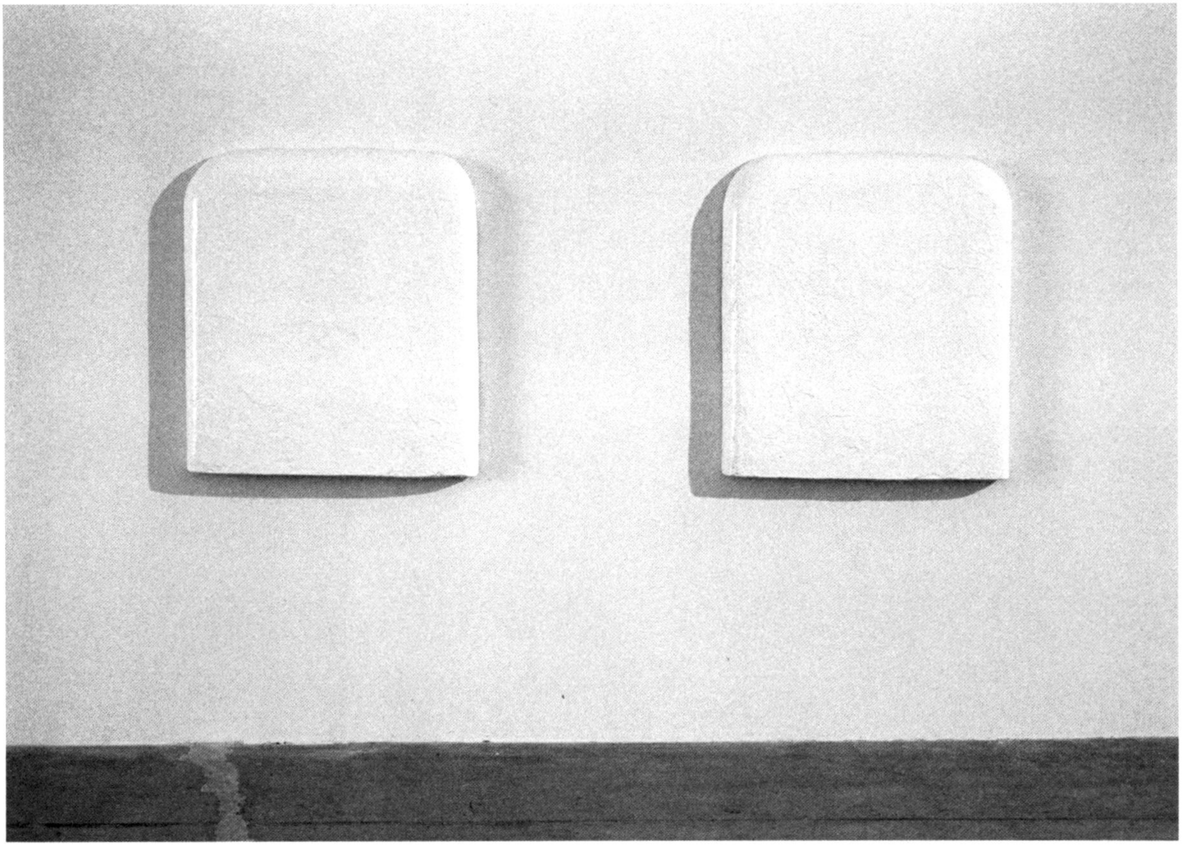

Robert Gober
A Pair of Basinless Sinks (1986)
Plaster, wood, wire lath,
semi-gloss enamel paint
68.6 x 168.9 x 6.6 cm

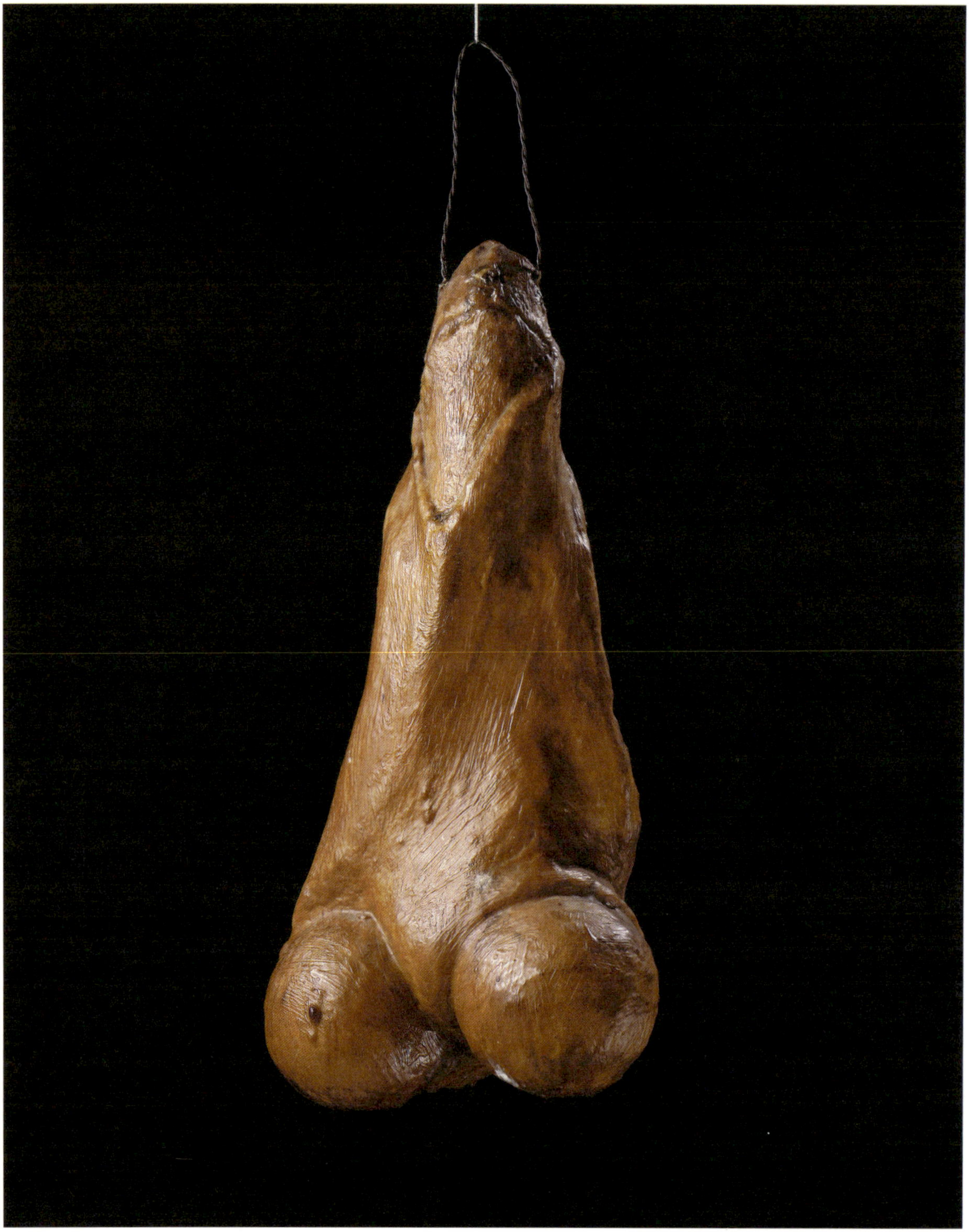

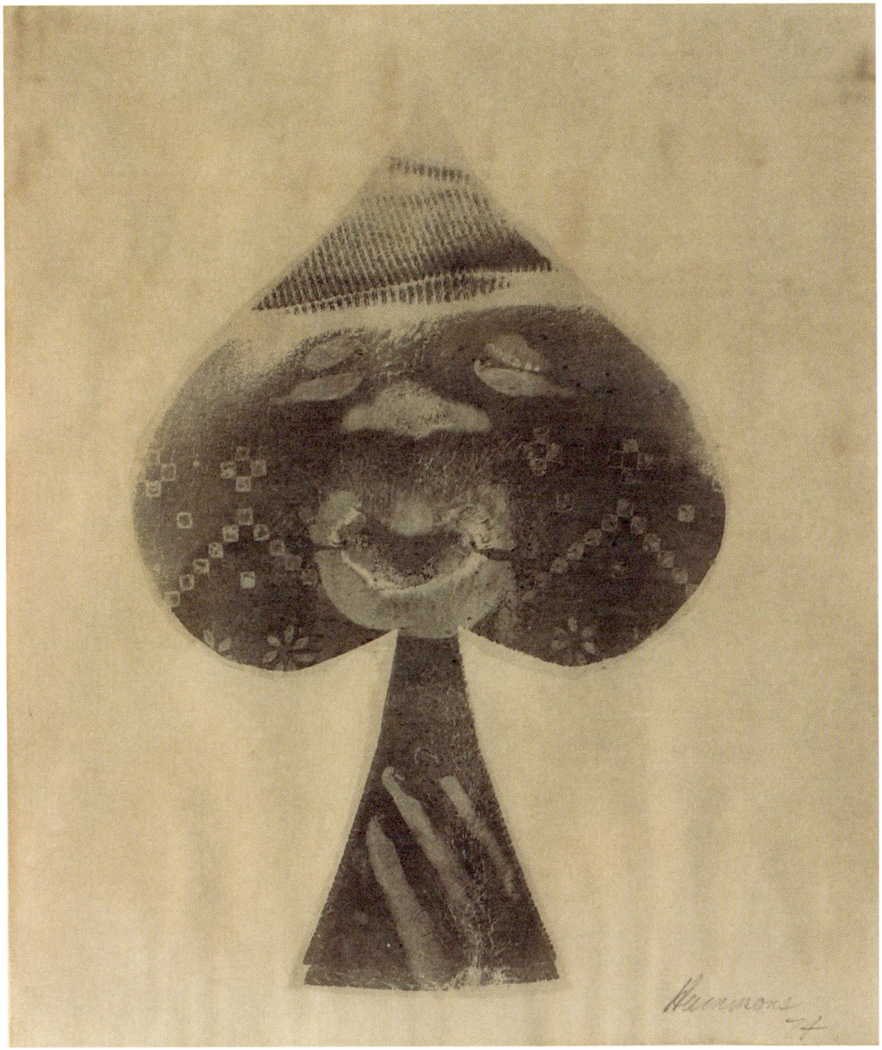

Louise Bourgeois
Fillette (Sweeter Version)
(1968–1999)
Latex over plaster
59.6 x 26.6 x 19.6 cm

David Hammons
Untitled (1974)
Body print
34.3 x 29.2 cm

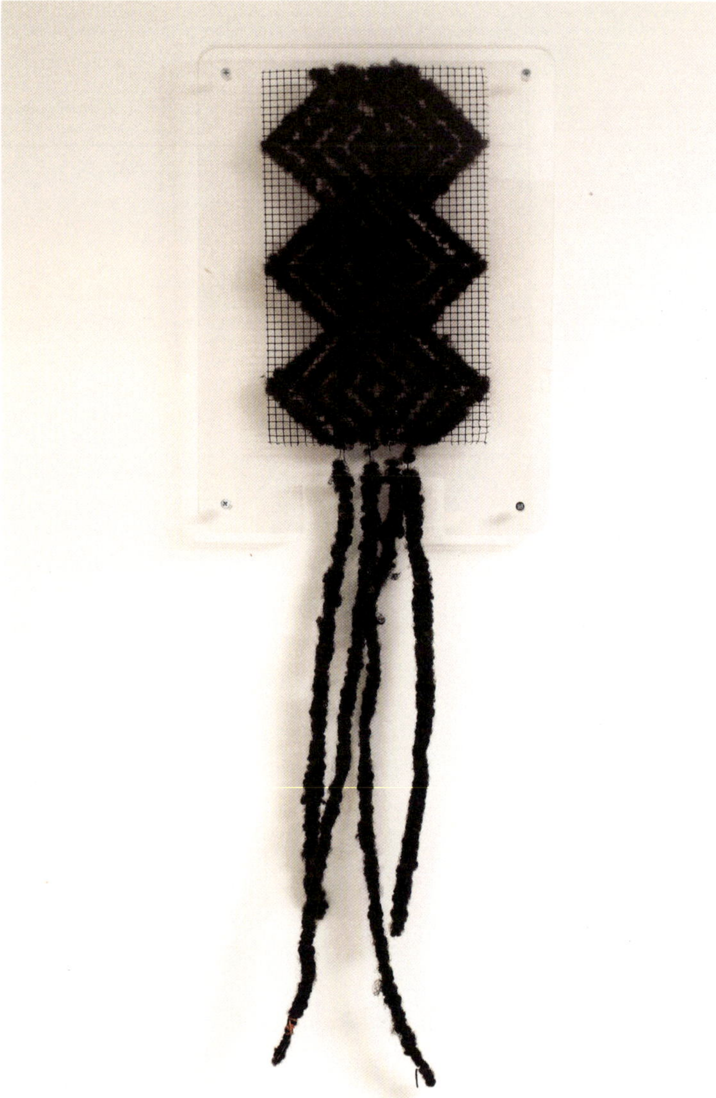

David Hammons
Untitled (Hair Piece)
(1975–1976)
Wire, hair
97.8 x 31.8 cm

David Hammons
Untitled (1975)
Body print
106.7 x 78.7 cm

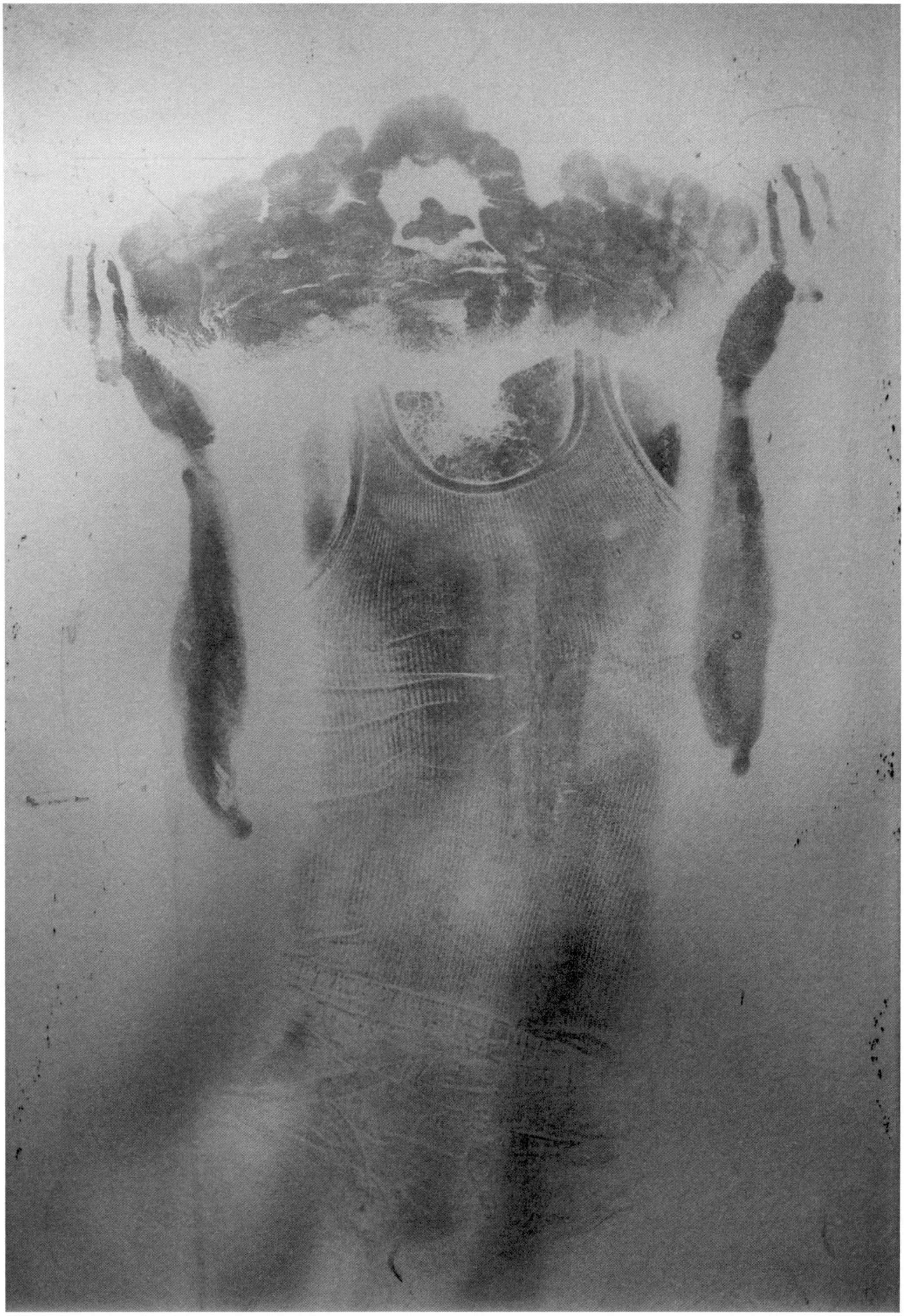

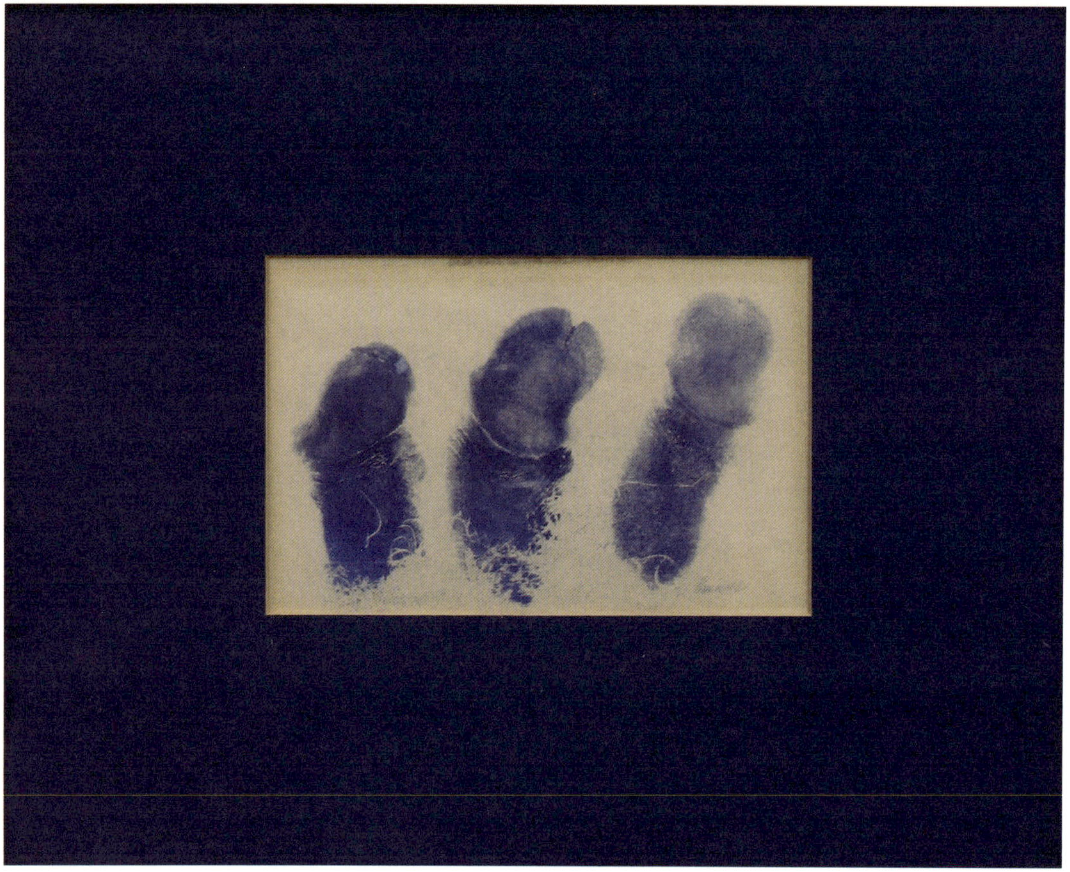

David Hammons
Blue Angels (Penises) (c.1970s)
Body print
29.7 x 37.7 cm

Jim Hodges
Untitled (Everything So Alive Lively Living) (2006)
Ink saliva transfer on paper
152.4 x 111.8 cm

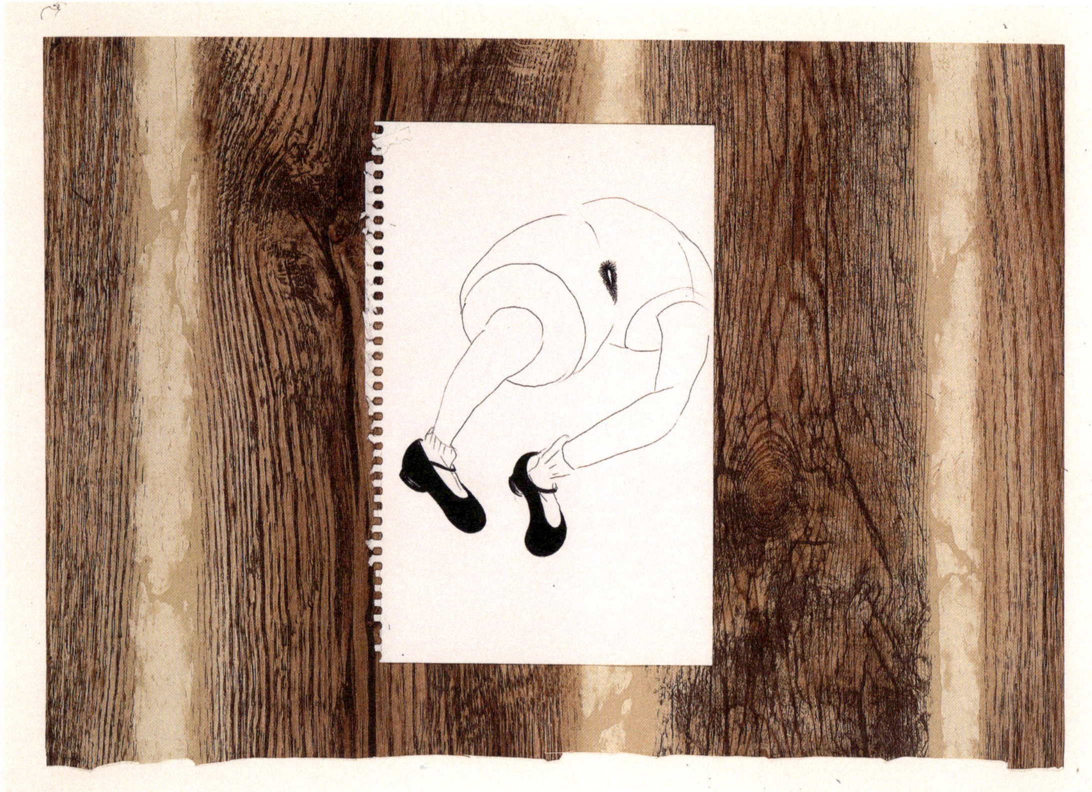

Sue Williams
Family Room (1994)
Ink on white paper from spiral block, collage on printed paper
30 x 44 cm

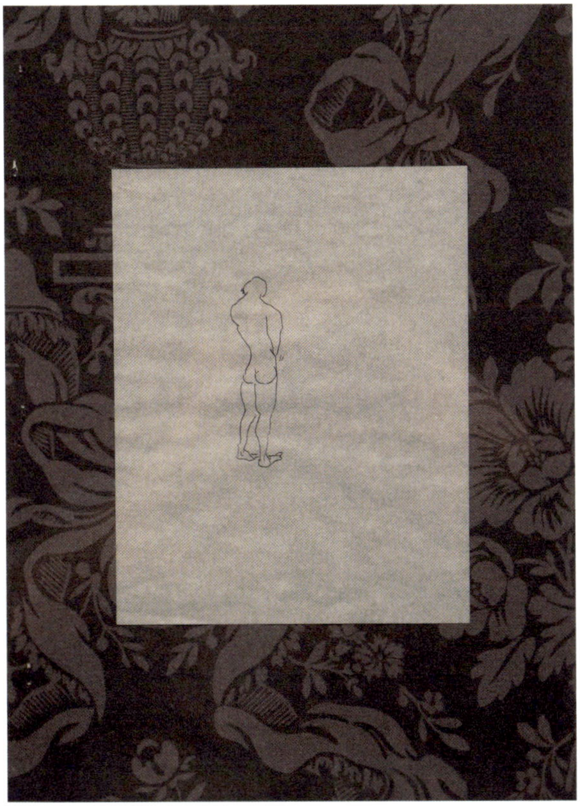

Busy With Calm Background (1995)
Ink on white paper, collage on wallpaper
44.5 x 33 cm

Creamy Floral (1995)
Ink on wallpaper
44.5 x 33 cm

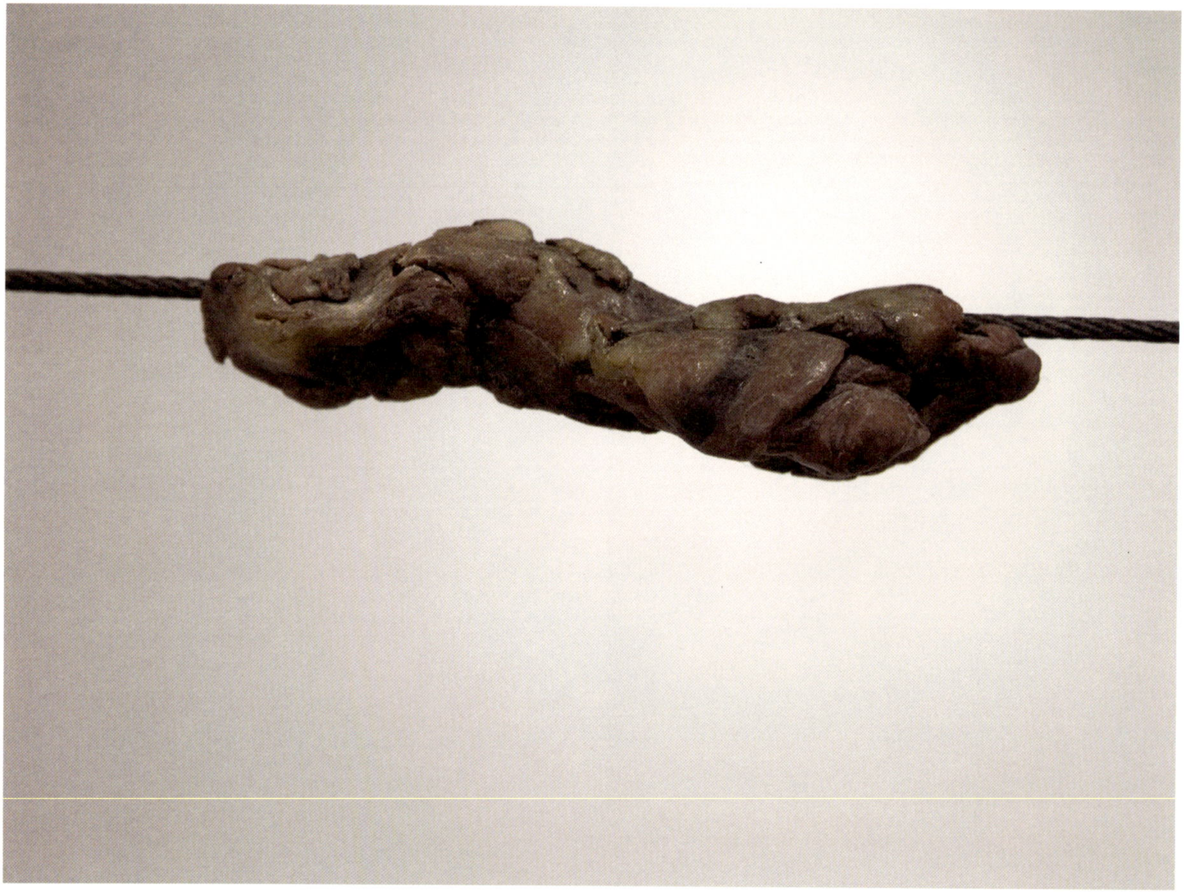

Paul Thek
Untitled (Meat Cable) (1969)
Wax, paint, steel cables
with turnbuckles
Length: 345.5 cm
Detail and installation view

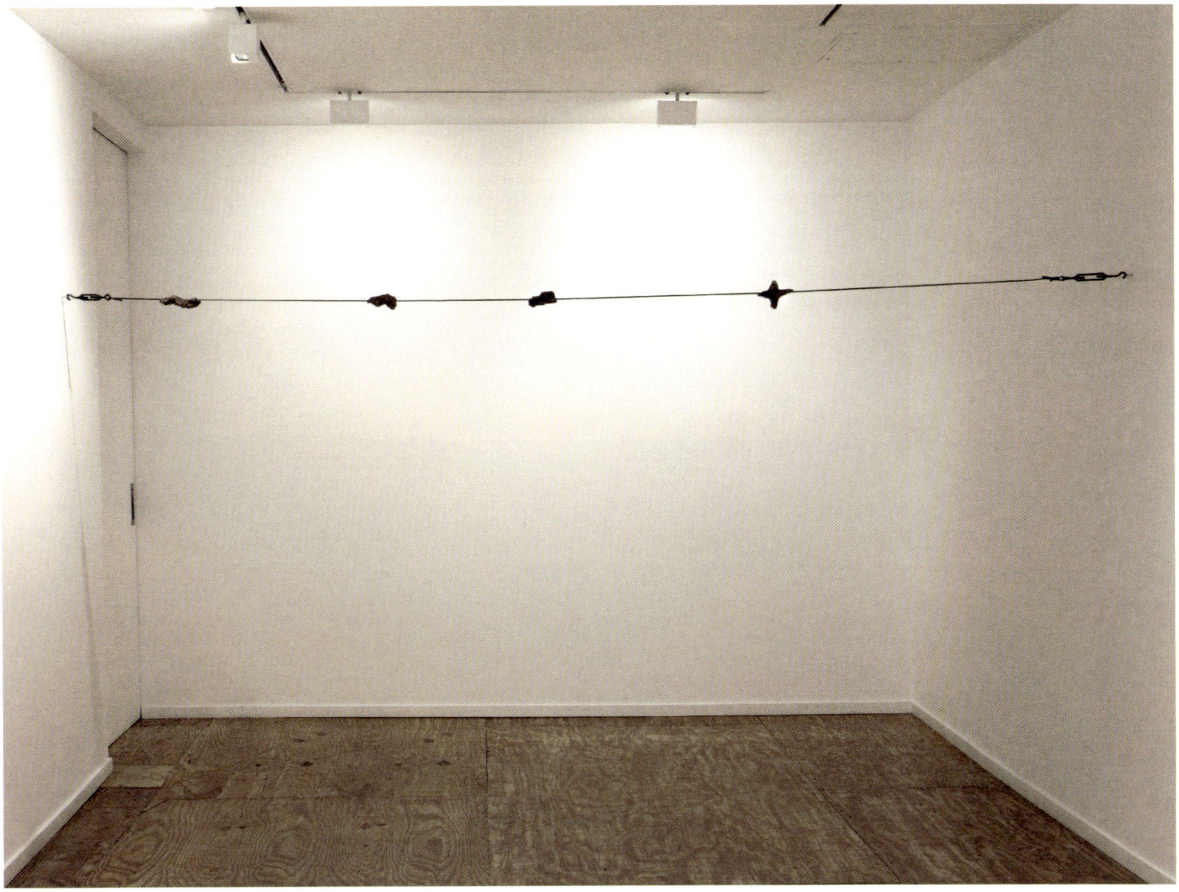

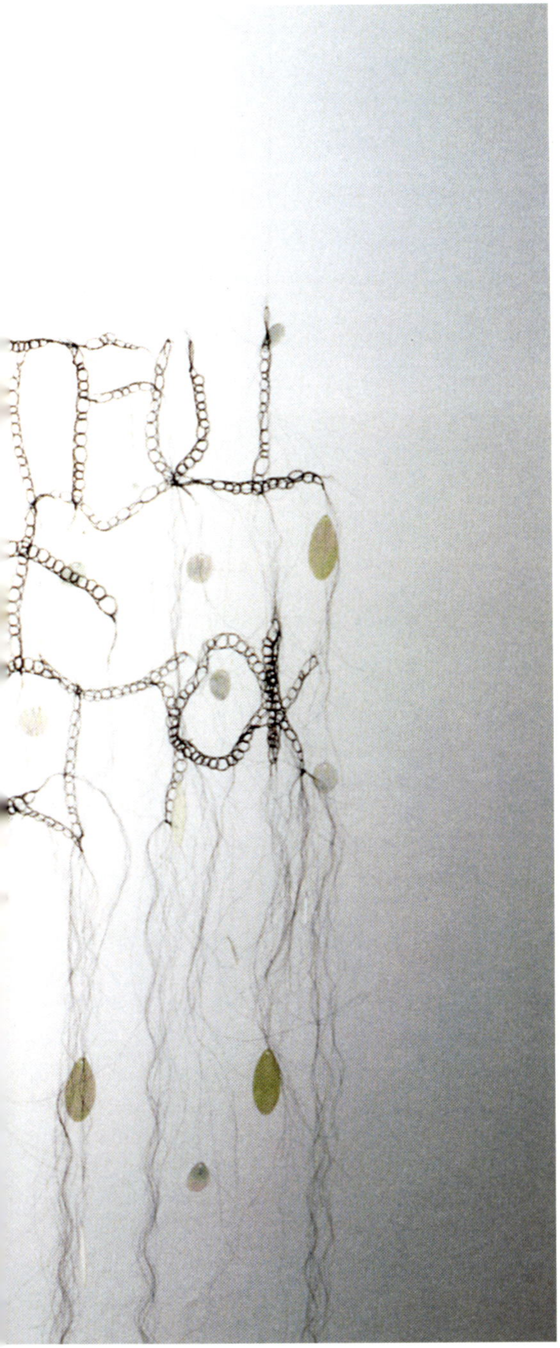

Despina Isaia
Untitled (2003)
Crochet with the artist's hair, sequins
75 x 100 cm

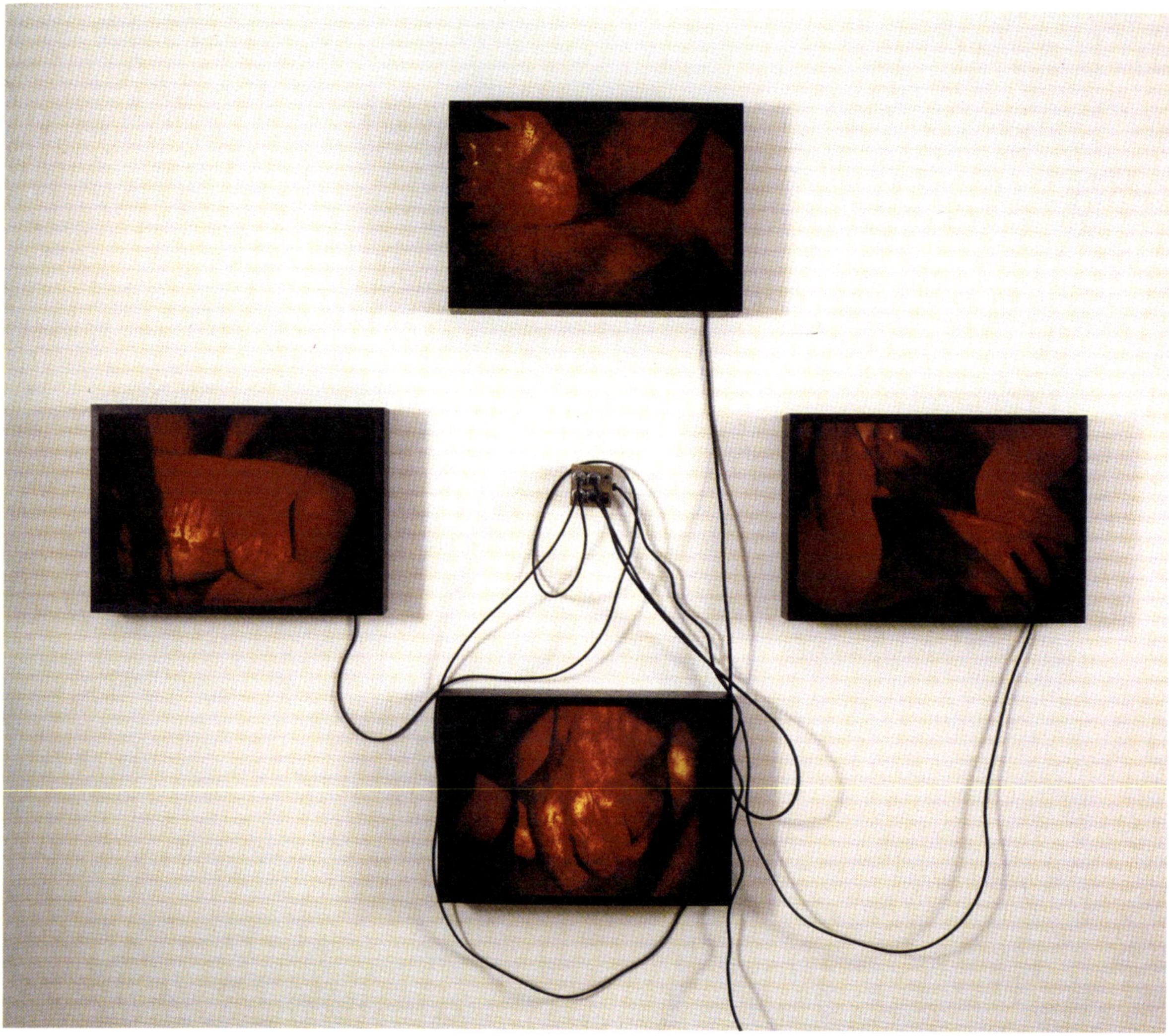

Kiki Smith
Untitled (1980–92)
Four lightboxes
Dimensions variable

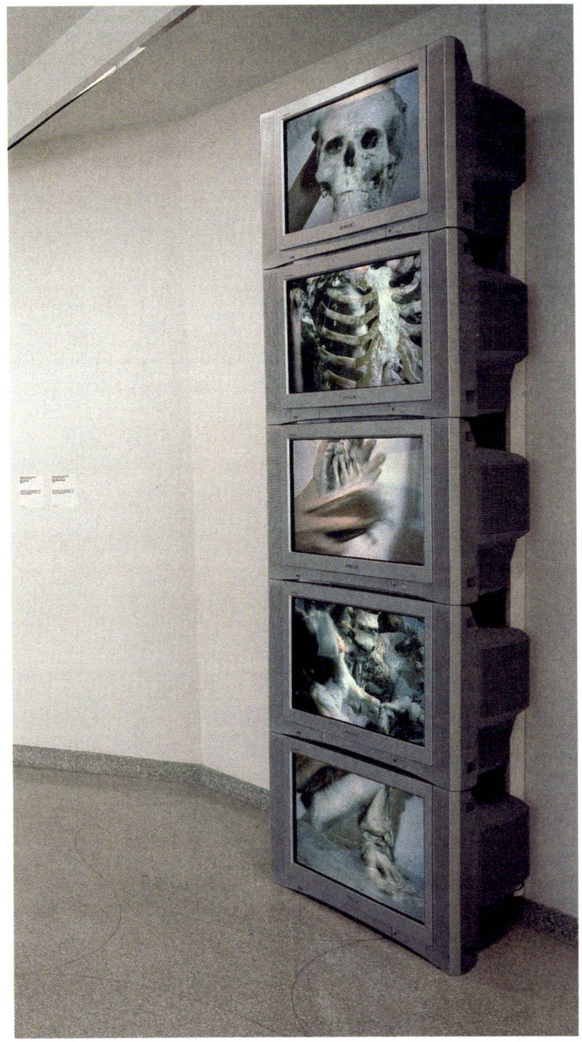

Marina Abramović
Cleaning the Mirror #1 (1995)
Video installation with
5 television monitors
Dimensions variable

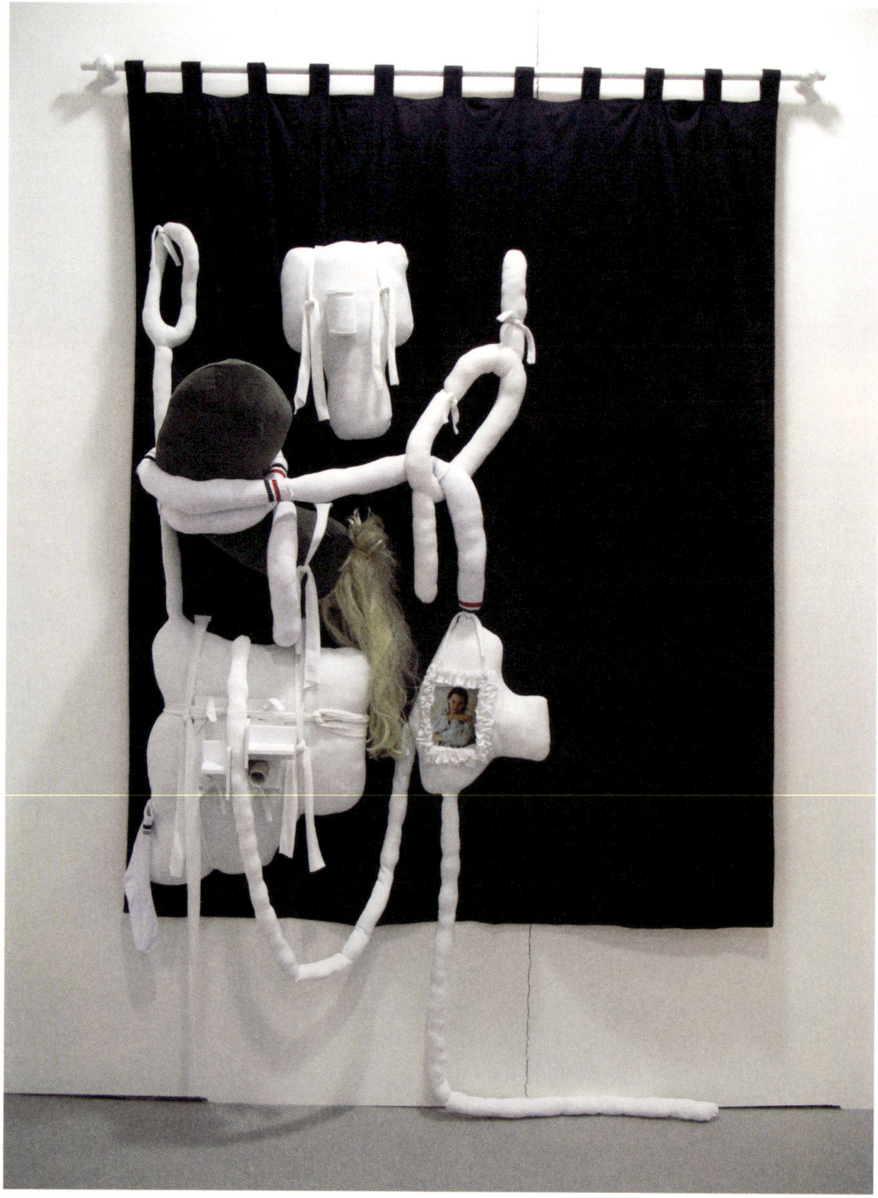

John Bock
Winona Ryder (2009)
Curtain with several objects
250 x 200 cm

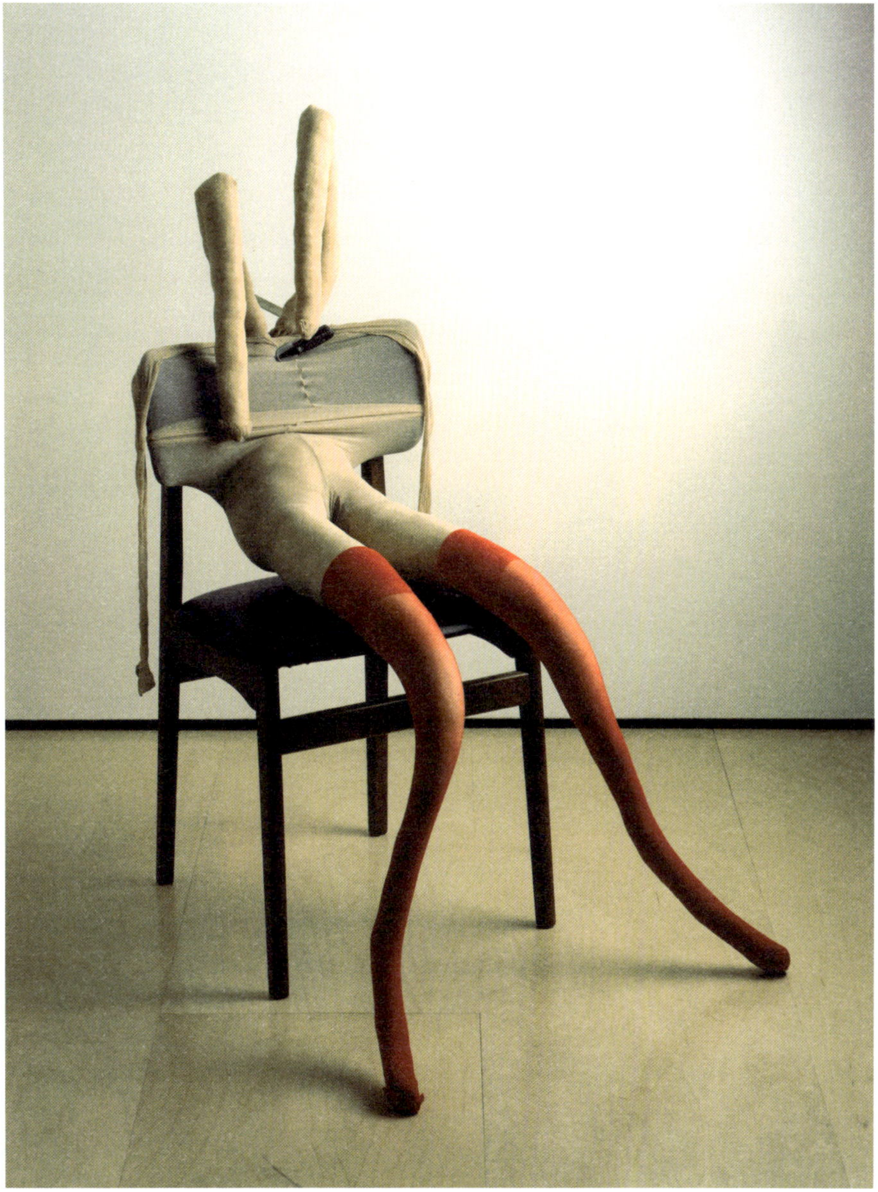

Sarah Lucas
Bunny Gets Snookered #10 (1997)
Tan tights, red stockings, chair,
steel clamp, kapok, wire
104 x 71 x 89 cm

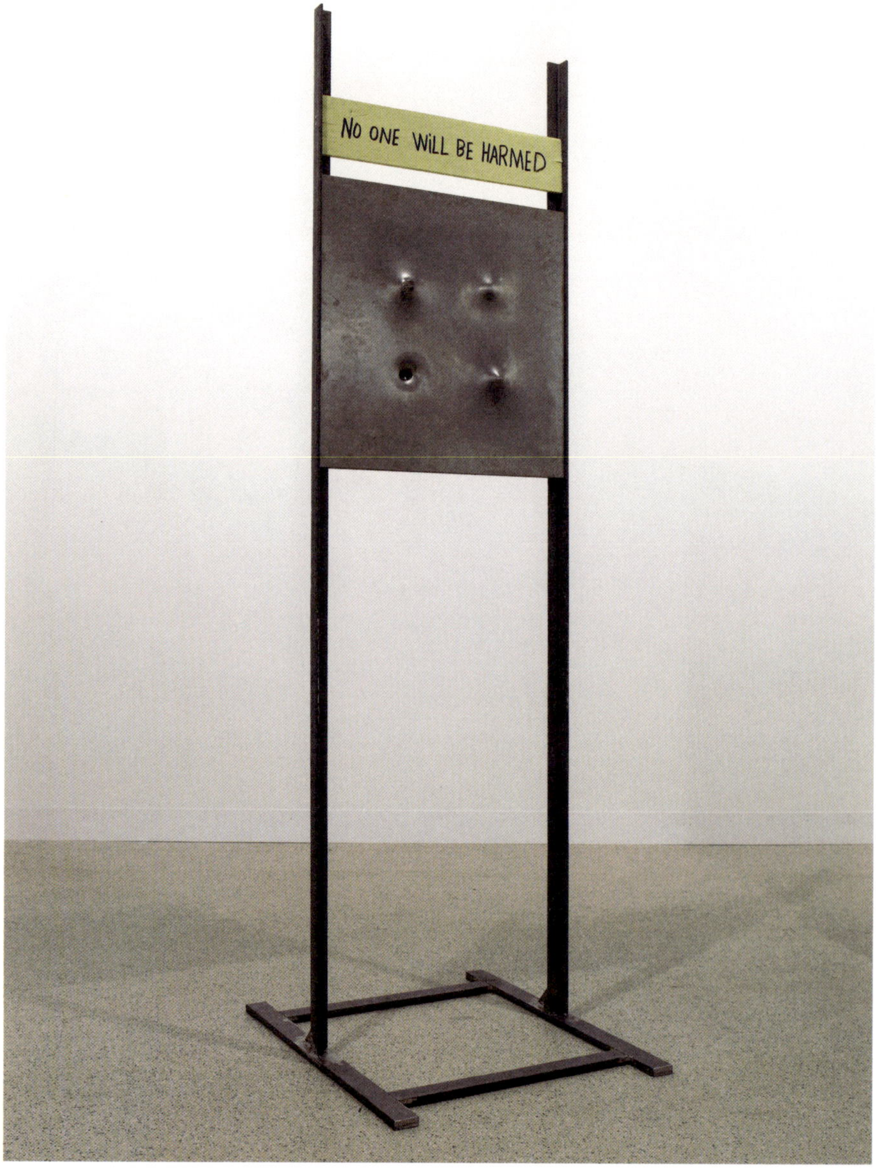

Jimmie Durham
No one will be harmed. This is only a test. (2008)
Metal, wood
180 x 51 x 65 cm

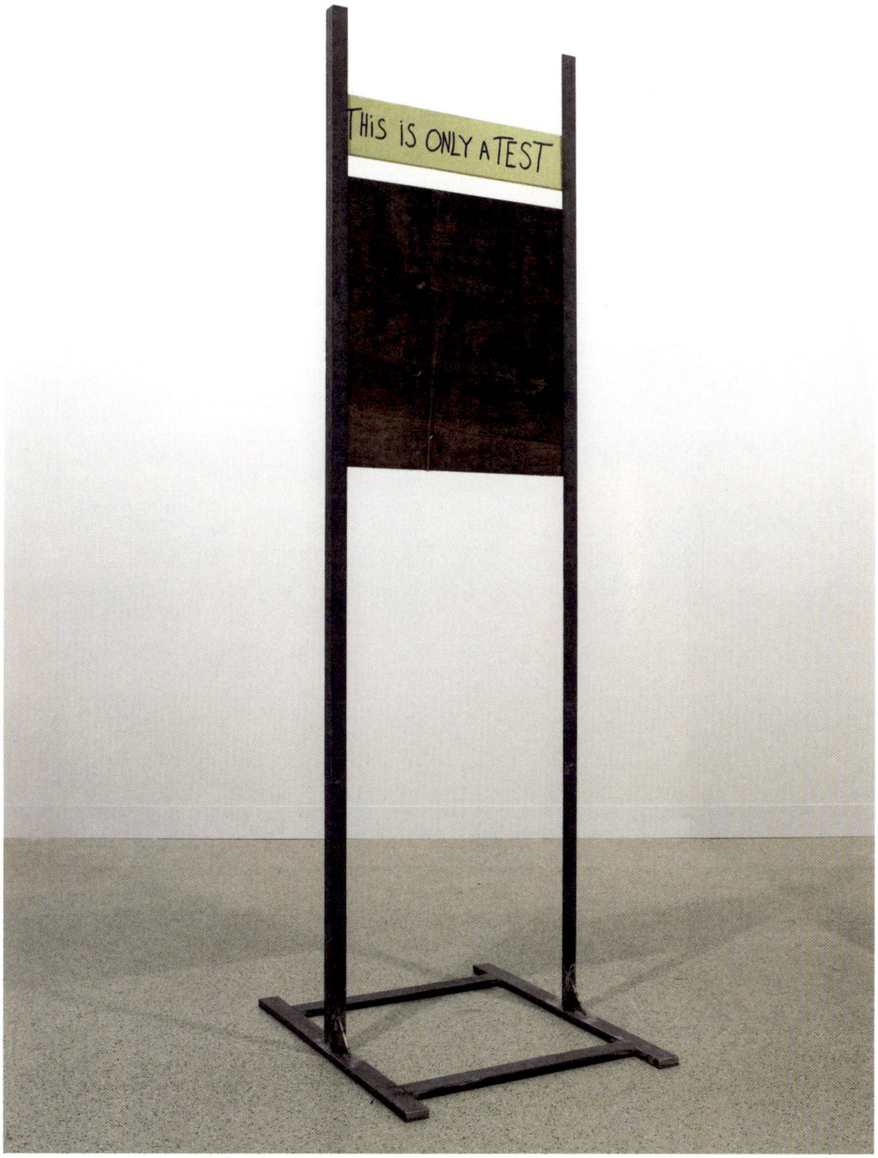
THIS IS ONLY A TEST

Subversive Abstraction

Act 2

Subversive Abstraction

I think distinctions between painting and sculpture are meaningless now. The real questions are: What is a work of art? What is the meaning behind the abstraction? What is it doing to me?
Lynda Benglis[1]

The discussion about the continuous validity of painting as a practice and whether this could still occupy a meaningful place within the rapidly changing social and cultural spheres of the twentieth century was central to many of the historic avant-garde movements. At the beginning of the century, Picasso and Braque's Cubism radically altered the understanding of the representational gambit, emphasising the autonomous nature of pictorial reality by way of fracturing the picture's surface. Soon after, their more extreme progenies such as Dada went so far as to declare the whole model of painting obsolete.

The model of abstraction which evolved from Cubism and the rich terrain for philosophical speculation this afforded, was key to a newly radicalised conceptualisation of painting. Abstraction allowed for a heightened degree of self-reflection with the debate around painting being tantamount to a more generic questioning of the continued relevance of art to society at large. Much of the early twentieth-century experiments with abstract forms, such as Malevich's Suprematist paintings or Mondrian's grids, for instance, sought to embody the utopian belief in social progress. The tragedies of World War II and the Holocaust rendered the notion of such progress a travesty. It was not until the 1950s that a group of US artists tried to rescue the avant-garde's faith in abstraction by infusing it with an American sense of scale. Referred to as Abstract Expressionists, painters such as Jackson Pollock, Mark Rothko and Barnett Newman developed a painterly idiom that sought to transcend ordinary reality and instead to create what they called 'a place'. However, to many younger artists critically engaged with contemporary culture their approach soon appeared unsatisfactory. In 1965, Donald Judd wrote: 'The main thing wrong with painting is that it is a rectangular plane placed flat against the wall. A rectangle is a shape itself; it is obviously the whole shape; it determines and limits the arrangement of whatever is on or inside of it.'[2] Judd's thoughts fed into Minimalism's preoccupation with phenomenology, which further emphasised the autonomy of the art object, especially in its reliance on the white cube of the institutional gallery space.

At the same time, a number of voices which had hitherto been marginal to the discussion around painting and abstraction, especially those of women and non-white artists, began to make an altogether different proposition by experimenting with painting, to borrow Rosalind Krauss' term, 'in an expanded field'.[3] They contested that painting was primarily defined by the idea of constructing an image, focusing instead on the materiality of painting – support, surface, painterly medium and relationship to wall. In their focus on the physical object they freed abstraction from its historically metaphysical demands and tied it closely to concrete preoccupations with everyday life.

Lynda Benglis was one of a group of artists working in New York during the late 1960s and early 1970s who pursued a new type of experimental abstract painting. This was fuelled by a somewhat ironic engagement with the history of Abstract Expressionism and its myth of the solitary male painter engaged in existential combat with his medium. Benglis was especially interested in process, as well as in re-establishing the directness of the medium by foregrounding its materiality. She did so by using a wide variety of unusual materials including wax, latex, polyurethane foam and sprayed metal. Garishly coloured, these were poured directly onto the gallery floor or squeezed into heaps doing away with the idea of a painting being displayed upright on a gallery wall.

Informed by her feminist studies, Benglis began in the 1970s to make video works which in an irreverent way exposed female stereotypes and traditional gender roles. This interest in the body is also apparent in her engagement with painting. The thickness of the limb-like tube in *Très* (1976), for example, references the proportions of the artist's arm. This has been shaped into an irregular form akin to a knot, ending in an emphatic horizontal movement. The final object undermines any discernable distinctions between colour, surface and support. Sprayed evenly in metal paint, as though it were a flat surface, *Très* engages in a sophisticated dynamic between painterly two- and sculptural three-dimensionality. Earlier aspirations towards the sublime have given way to a play with abjection that led curator and critic, Richard Marshall to describe Benglis' early knotted paintings as 'nausea balls'.[4]

Tensions between painterly and sculptural paradigms also inform Robert Gober's *Unfolding Door* (1989). When seen head on, the work appears to be a highly stylised composition of vertical fields and a central horizontal volume. The austerity and formal rigour are reminiscent of early Constructivist schema. However, on closer inspection the object, which is displayed like a painting, reveals itself to be a wooden household door that in an absurd motion twists on itself. This treatment plays with the defining properties of what makes a door 'a door'(and what makes a painting 'a painting', for that matter): it is neither flat nor opens, nor does it offer transit or demarcate a clear line of separation. Where easel painting since the Renaissance has been understood as a window offering a view onto an imaginary world – think of Alberti or Dürer's diagrammatic renditions of the painter surveying his subject through a picture frame – Gober's dysfunctional door bars any access to a world beyond the surface. The cross form is a recurring motive in Gober's oeuvre – it figures prominently, for instance, in his trademark plugs – and is a direct allusion to his Catholic heritage and the Christian iconography of suffering. Playing on the double-meaning of 'painting' – as in painting a picture or decorating – *Unfolding Door* undermines the historically elevated status of painting as a medium. Laden with uncanny symbolism, this surreal object negates the metaphysical ideals often associated with abstraction.

The use of unorthodox materials, especially those with connotations of waste and dirt, is also central to the work of David Hammons.[5] *Flight Fantasy* (1995) is one of the most impressive examples from a body of works whose title denotes the possibility of rising above the limitations of day-to-day reality. Hammons realised the first work in the series in his studio in 1975 in Los Angeles before moving to New York's Harlem. The present version was originally conceived for A Gathering of the Tribes, a gallery on New York's Lower East side founded in 1991 by Steve Cannon, a former professor at City University, New York and close friend of Hammons.

In *Flight Fantasy* Hammons mobilises the language of abstraction to question its relationship to Modernism's preoccupation with hygiene and to the emphatic rationalism of the Enlightenment project (with slavery and colonialism as its dark and repressed flipside). Hammons' painting is executed directly on the wall – not unlike the wall paintings of Daniel Buren, Sol LeWitt or Niele Toroni – thus breaking down the traditional distinction between painting as an art and painting as interior decoration. Rejecting the fetishism of the artist's touch, the paint is applied with rollers rather than a brush.

Loops of coiled wire threaded with locks of hair collected from barber's shops in Harlem break the image surface. Human hair has long been associated with notions of the abject. The luxurious red paint, the gold pattern reminiscent of elegant wallpapers and the reflective crystals are all anathema to Modernism's preoccupation with clean surfaces. Hammons purchased the rollers for the pattern during a sojourn in Vienna, the city where Adolf Loos, in 1908 published his manifesto of modern architecture, *Ornament and Crime*, in which he called for the elimination of ornament from all useful objects. Through this sophisticated use of 'anti-modernist' elements, Hammons reclaims signifiers of social and cultural exclusion, not least painting itself, for those customarily sidelined by the rhetoric of Western art.

The same applies to Kori Newkirk and his use of braided hair and pony beads in his curtain 'paintings' although his approach is less deterministic. Born in New York's Bronx and working in Los Angeles, Newkirk has described his work as 'ghetto-fabulous conceptualism'.[6] The politics of identity are implicit in the material and its associations with the styling of afro-hair. Similarly to Hammons, Newkirk combines a sophisticated use of materials with an exceedingly elegant formal vocabulary, thus creating an ambiguity that prevents the work from falsely simplistic readings. Hovering between allusions to landscape painting and abstraction, *Virgil* (2002) enters into a rich dialogue with the traditions of US post-war painting. At the same time the curtain entails a destabilising element. Rather than open a view onto a world beyond, it could be parted and walked through to reveal that there is nothing behind, thus returning it to the mundane world of the everyday from which it is borrowed.

A combination of potentially abject materials and instability also informs the work of Dieter Roth whose practice is rooted in an entirely different context. Born in 1930, Roth initially trained in Switzerland as a graphic designer where he was exposed to the teachings of concrete art, especially the Zurich Group around Max Bill and Camille Graeser. From the mid-1950s onwards he worked in a strictly geometrical abstract idiom. However, following his relocation to Iceland in 1957 and subsequent docent appointment at the Rhode Island School of Design in Providence, his aesthetic dramatically changed. Whilst in Providence, he incorporated for the first time food, namely chocolate, into one of his prints. Food with its unpredictable material qualities was soon to play an increasingly important role in his work.

Small Landscape (Kleine Landschaft) (1969) and *Large Landscape (Grosse Landschaft)* (1969) are made by pressing cheese onto paper and roofing felt respectively, preserving the final arrangement between layers of plastic sheets. The materials' perishable qualities have a discernable impact on the work's composition and its final appearance, particularly as regards colouration and contrast. Roth was keen to integrate decay in the process of

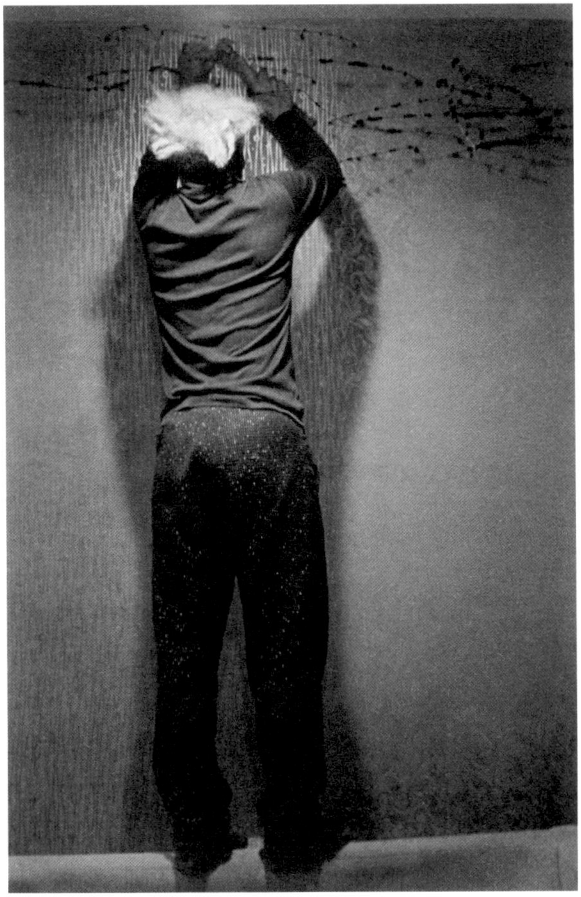

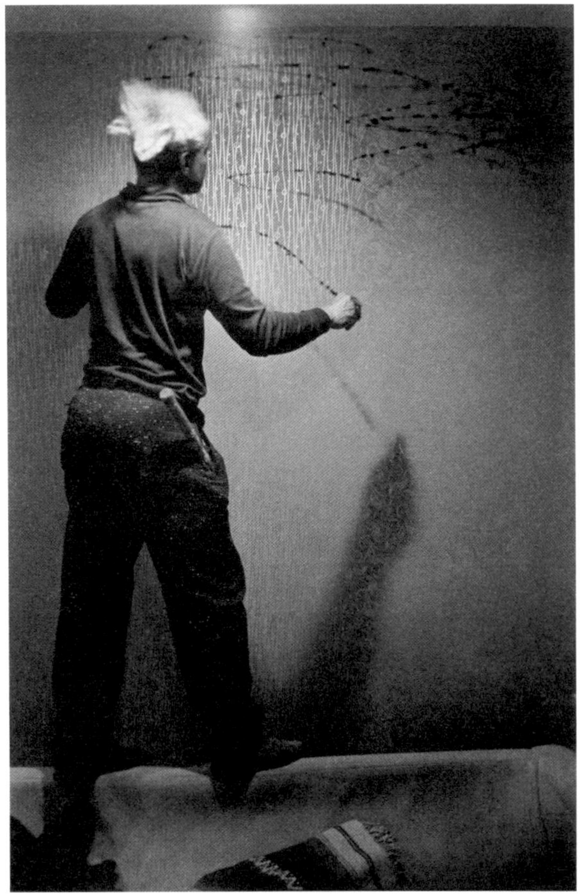

John Ranard
NYC-35-95-David Hammons (1995)
David Hammons installing
Flight Fantasy (1995)
Installation from A Gathering
of the Tribes Gallery
Silver gelatin fibre
Exhibition photographic prints
Each 27.9 x 35.6cm
(Above and overleaf)

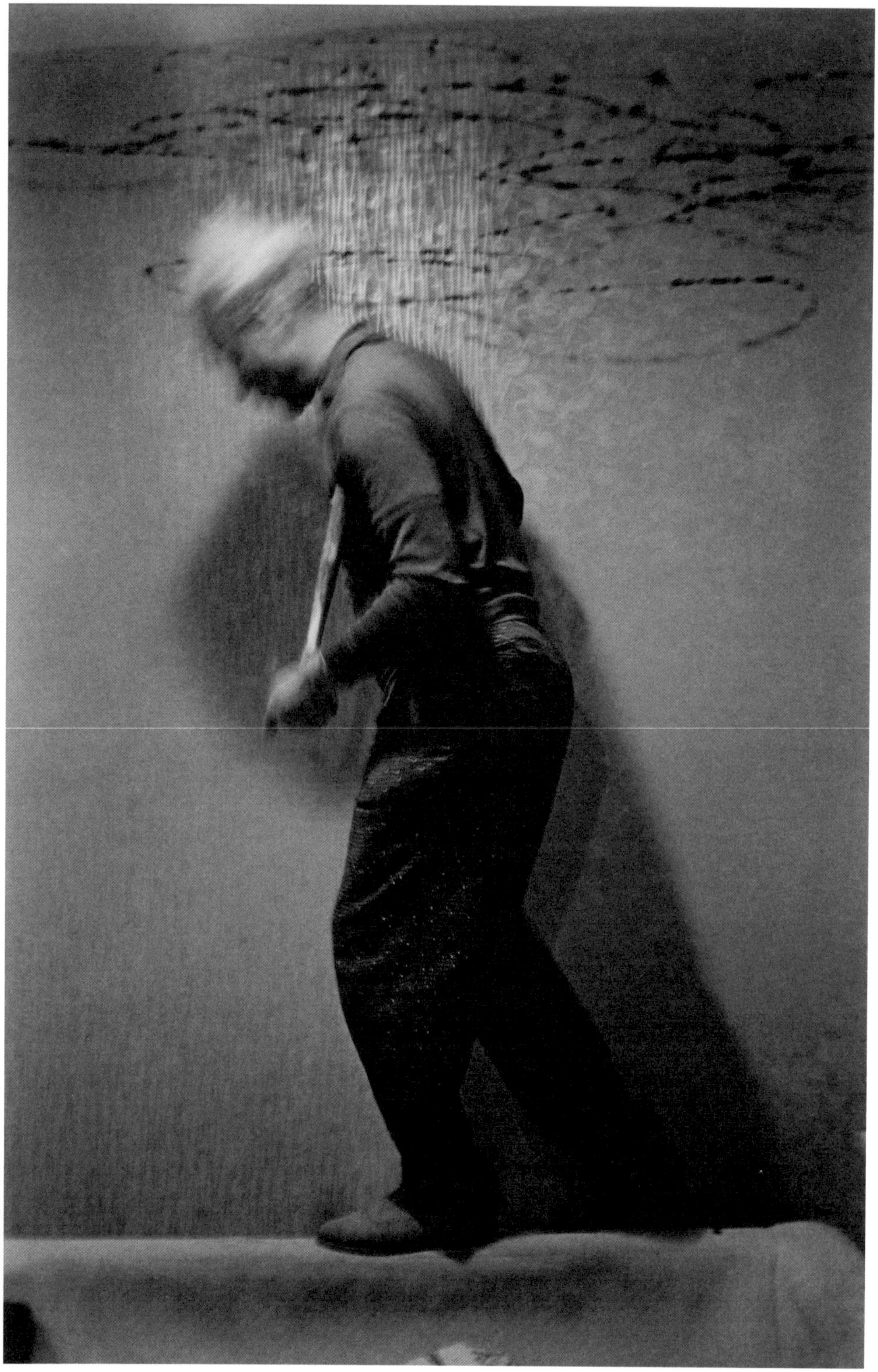

creation, not least to make play with his own limitations and failures as an artist. Even without the title, the implied horizon line and the circle are sufficient to suggest such motifs as landscape and sunrise. The materiality of these works is inescapable, it constantly reasserts itself. They are insistent on being part of this world and refuse any metaphysical aspirations. In this they are close to the spirit of *Nouveau Réalisme* or New Realism, an art movement founded in 1960 by the art critic Pierre Restany and the painter Yves Klein, for which Roth claimed a great sense of affinity.

The artists associated with *Nouveau Réalisme* aspired to bring art and life closer together and to do so by recycling debris from urban life and integrating this in an unmediated way into their work. Making extensive use of collage and assemblage techniques they blurred the lines between traditional medium categories. Nikos Kessanlis, though not an official member of the group, was closely aligned with its ethos. Greek by birth, but at the time resident in Paris, he produced between 1960 and 1962 a series of works called *Gestures*, which were largely composed of quotidian objects the artist found in his studio. The title alludes to the importance of the artistic gesture as the decisive act which by combining materials in unorthodox juxtapositions can open new spaces of meaning. *Gesture* (1961) consists of a toilet cistern suspended upside down from which flows a crumpled cloth weighed down by the cistern's lid. The work entails a number of formal juxtapositions such as inside and out, hard and soft, heavy and light, while being united by the overall lack of colour. The cloth metaphorically adopts the qualities of water and introduces an element of dynamic movement while also giving the sculptural arrangement an air of painting in space.

The Nouveaux Réalistes' use of materials was historically indebted to the spirit of Dada and anti-art. While proclaiming the death of art on the one hand, Dada on the other advocated that absolutely everything could be turned into art. Dada's irreverent and highly original use of everyday materials reverberates in an early collage by Damien Hirst. Atypical for Hirst's work, it nonetheless shows his longstanding rejection of the divide between art and life, albeit in a way that is heavily indebted to historic antecedents such as the assemblages of Kurt Schwitters.

Rosemarie Trockel also cites Schwitters as one of her influences.[7] Though working in a great variety of media including drawing, film, video, sculpture, installation and performance, and eschewing a signature style, all of Trockel's work is imbued with a highly attuned material sensibility. Many of her objects defy easy categorisation and obstreperously resist linguistic definition. *Avalanche* (2008), for instance, one moment looks like an austere hybrid between painting and sculpture, the next like a craft object with no clear purpose, and finally like a dysfunctional sink.

From her early knitted pictures to her tableaux of stove plates, Trockel has looked to the domestic for inspiration. The domestic sphere, traditionally female, is often seen as antithetical to the public, male arena. A similar dichotomy is implicit in the value judgements attached to art and the crafts, not least in the history of Modernism (one should not forget, for instance, that however progressive the Bauhaus may have been, it did not admit women to its painting classes but only to its craft workshops). This interest in craft and its potential for developing a new language of abstraction is also inherent in *Avalanche* and Trockel's idiosyncratic use of ceramics.

Avalanche is reliant on a set of stark formal contrasts: white versus black, shiny versus dull, firm and attached versus suspended and mobile. This predilection for contrasts, which, rather than being resolved, relish the ambiguity they create, also characterises *Something Of Tomorrow I* (2008). The work adopts all the tropes of conventional painting: ground, surface, frame and glazing. However each component transgresses customary boundaries: the Perspex sheet overshoots the frame, the frame connects to the support, paint is applied graffiti style with the final composition, a combination of controlled action and gravitational pull on the running spray paint. The final result is characterised by a taut dynamic between controlled formalism and disconcerting formlessness that straddles the spectrum of abstraction and abjection.

The polarity of formalism and abjection is also central to Mike Kelley's *Transplant* (1990). In the spirit of Duchamp's ready-mades and Dada's anti-art, Kelley has arranged three geometrically patterned blankets in a rigorously composed line-up on the floor. Each blanket acts as a field with a clearly defined boundary, not unlike the canvas in a painting. Placed on either of the larger outer blankets is a soft toy. Toy animals first appeared in Kelley's work in the late 1980s. Acquired from second-hand shops, these redundant gate-keepers of childhood in their neutered, sexless state are reminders of a developmental phase which precedes the completion of the psycho-sexual cycle on which social conditioning is based. They also play on the notion of innocence which is based on the subtraction of anything that is directly reminiscent of bodily functions, a subtraction that also manifests itself in the Modernist preoccupation with hygiene and purity.

The prevalence of shades of brown with its connotations of faeces is a further allusion to the anal stages of childhood development, as is the display on the ground (rather than the wall), the direction of the abject. Altogether *Transplant* is a reminder of all that is deeply human and which resists the urge towards sublimation that is so important to the workings of abstraction. Elsewhere, Kelley has observed: 'My work is perched between these nostalgic assemblage artists on the one side and this classical commodity art on the other side. It's not about idealisation.'[8]

Collapse of a different kind characterises the large paintings and delicate drawings of Julie Mehretu. Mehretu draws on a wide variety of source material from architectural drawings to computer graphics, maps and quotations of historic models such as Russian Constructivism. Some of these make reference to Mehretu's biography – exiled from her native Ethiopia she grew up and studied in the US, and now divides her time between New York and Berlin – while others are the fruits of her tireless sampling of readily available imagery from a plethora of sources. The works mix media as much as they conflate representation and abstraction. The complex relationship between Mehretu's abstraction and its Modernist heritage expresses itself particularly in her sophisticated use of perspective with diagonal lines creating a sense of volume and space that runs counter to her historic predecessors' predilection for the grid to assert the flatness of the canvas. Instead, her paintings and drawings suggest a vortex that threatens to pull the rug out from under the viewer's feet.

Throughout the history of Modernism, abstraction, and especially the monochrome, has always entailed an element of the endgame, in which the notion of the void or nothingness has occupied a central role. Daniel Subkoff subverts this idea by taking the void as a starting point rather than a finishing line. Reverting to the performative aspects of painting Subkoff treats the bare canvas as raw material not to create an image but to splice up what conventionally is the support structure to create an installation that reaches out into the surrounding space. Subkoff was inspired by the memories of his grandfather, a war veteran, and the film *The Great Escape* (1968), in which prisoners of war use every meagre material at their disposal. He amalgamated these personal references with the wider question of what constitutes a painting: 'The resourcefulness of the escapees in the film compelled me to escape from the conventional processes and dimensions of painting, using the foundational materials themselves but abandoning both the old, late Modernist obsessions with paint and surface and the more recent fixation with doing away with the object altogether.'[9] *All Her Clothes Are Swept Aside by Her Face* (2008) borrows from the Duchampian strategy of further charging an object's meaning by giving it an enigmatic title, in this instance to capture the idea of movement and performance. Yet, the only visible actor is not the female of the title but the animated canvas itself. Far from a conclusion, the material and conceptual conventions of painting and abstraction are revealed here as open-ended in their newly liberated condition.

Notes

1 Erica-Lynn Huberty, 'Intensity of Form and Surface: An Interview with Lynda Benglis', *Sculpture Magazine*, July–August 2000, cited in R. Marshall, *Lynda Benglis* (New York: Cheim & Read, 2004) n.p.

2 Donald Judd, 'Specific Objects', in Charles Harrison and Paul Wood, eds., *Art in Theory: 1900–1990: An Anthology of Changing Ideas* (London: Blackwell Publishing Ltd., 1992) 809–813.

3 This notion is borrowed from Krauss' seminal essay, 'Sculpture in the Expanded Field', *October*, Spring 1979, 31–44. See also Katy Siegel, ed., *High Times, Hard Times: New York Painting 1967–1975* (New York: Independent Curators International, 2006).

4 Richard Marshall, *Lynda Benglis* (New York: Cheim and Read, 2004) n.p.

5 See also Chapter 1, *Keeping it Real* on David Hammons' *Body Prints*.

6 Kori Newkirk as cited in Karen Rosenberg, 'Raising Consciousness Beyond the Beaded Curtain', *New York Times*, 16 November 2007.

7 'Rosemarie Trockel talks to Isabelle Graw – '80s Then – Interview', *Artforum*, March 2003, 224.

8 Paul Taylor, 'Toying with Second-Hand Souvenirs', in Thomas Kellein, *Mike Kelley* (Basel: Kunsthalle Basel, 1992) 58.

9 From a personal statement by Daniel Subkoff, March 2010.

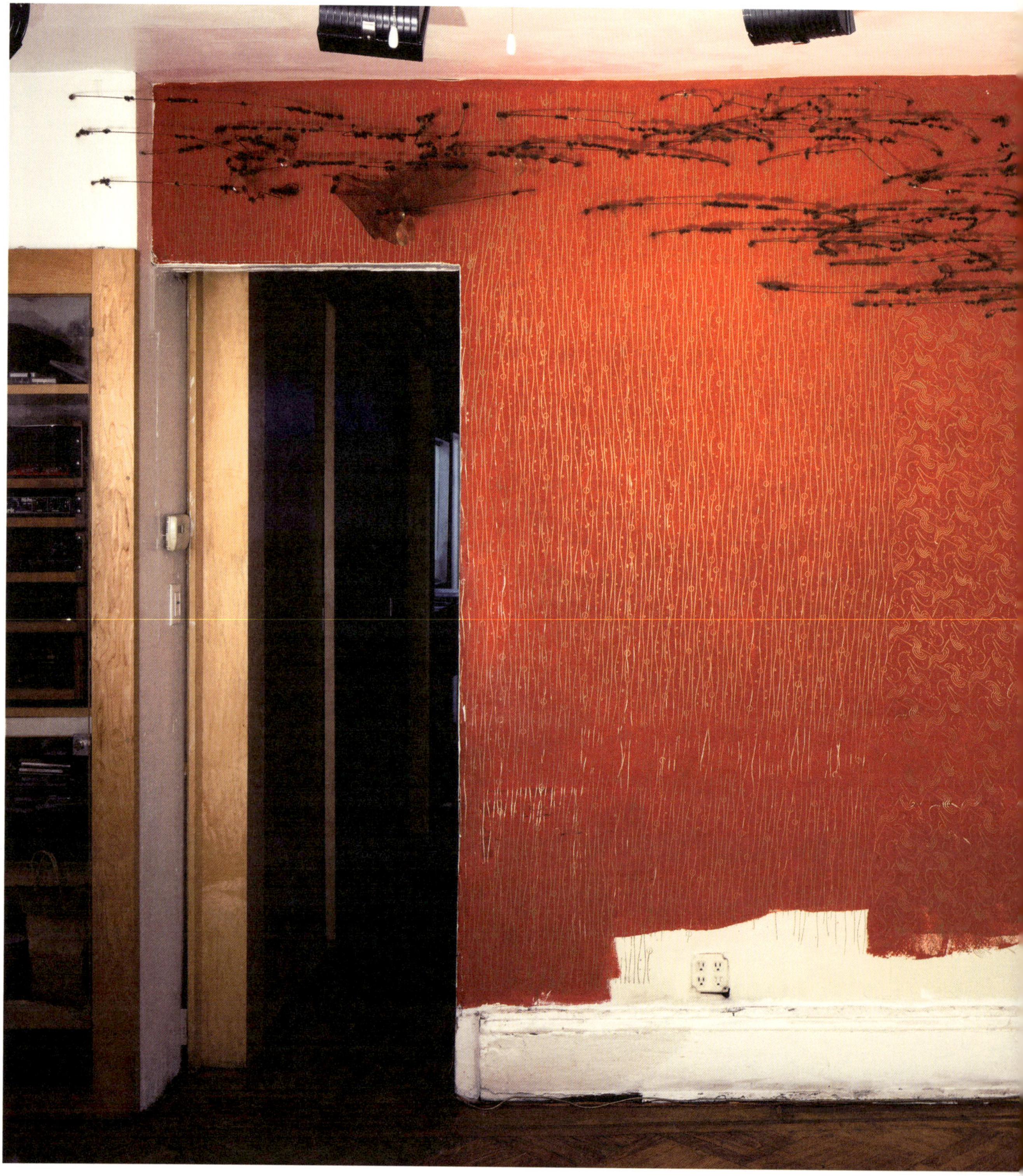

David Hammons
Flight Fantasy (1995)
Installation at A Gathering of the Tribes Gallery c.1995
Paint, custom rollers, heavy metal wire hoops, human hair, crystals, netting
365.8 x 243.8 cm

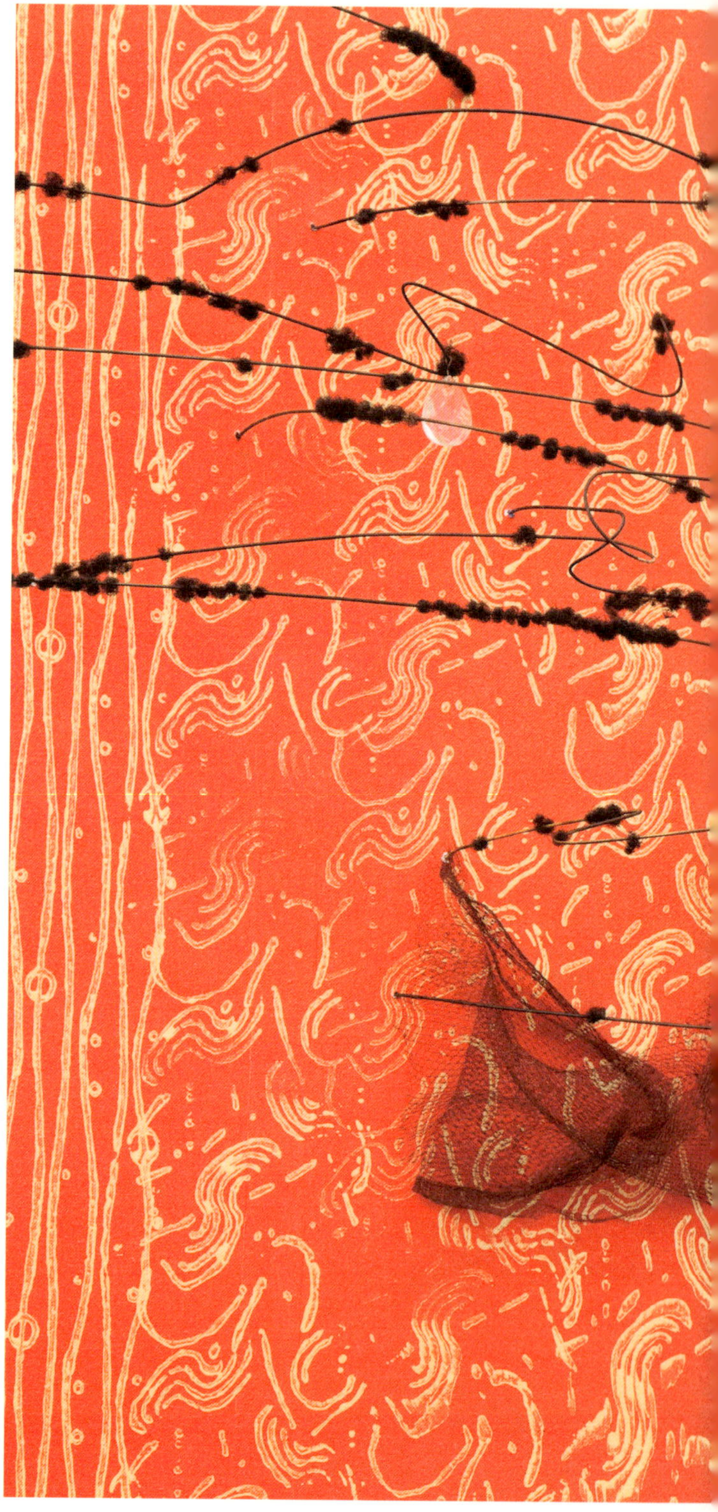

David Hammons
Flight Fantasy (1995)
Paint, custom rollers, heavy metal wire hoops, human hair, crystals, netting
365.8 x 243.8 cm
Detail

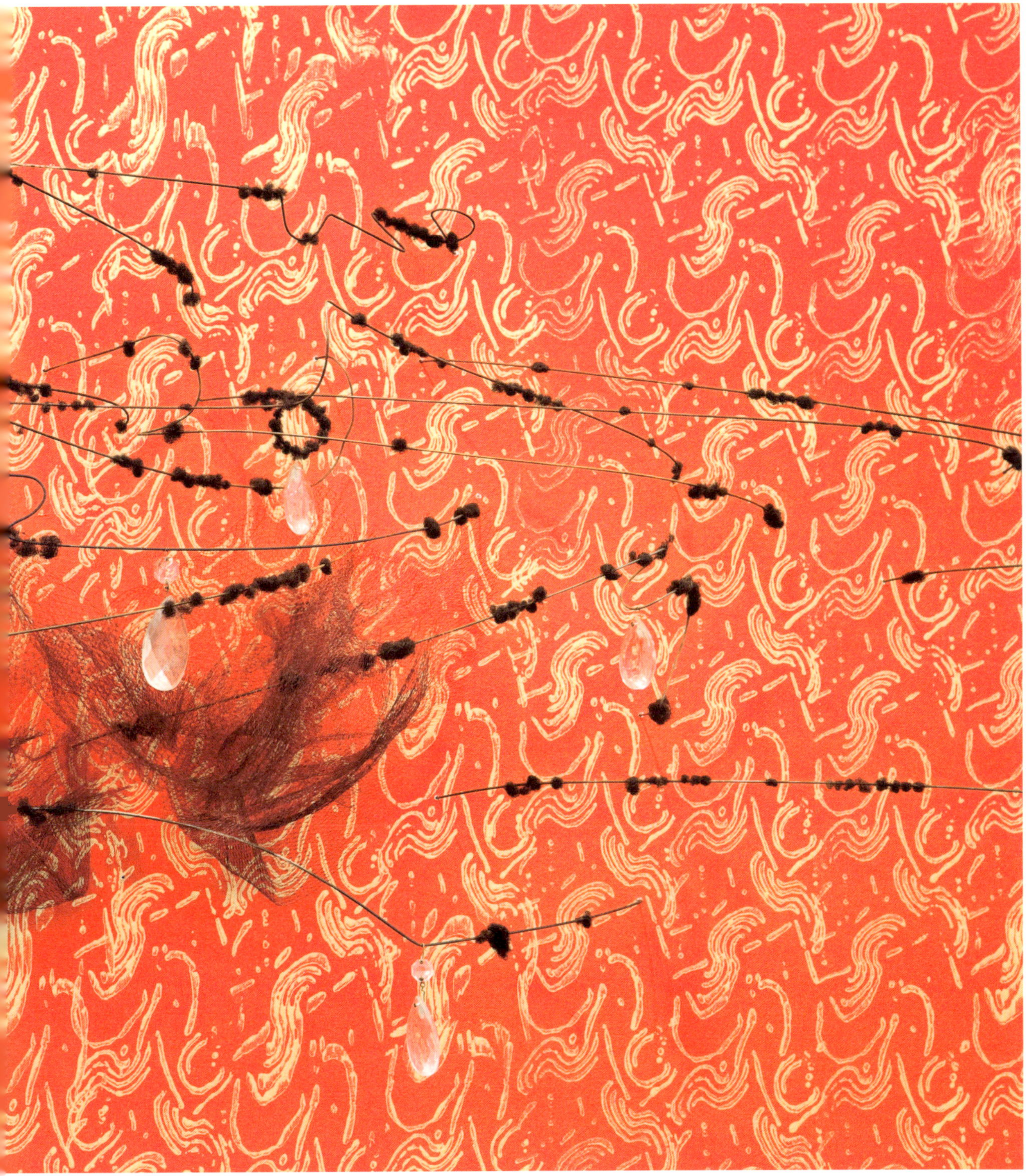

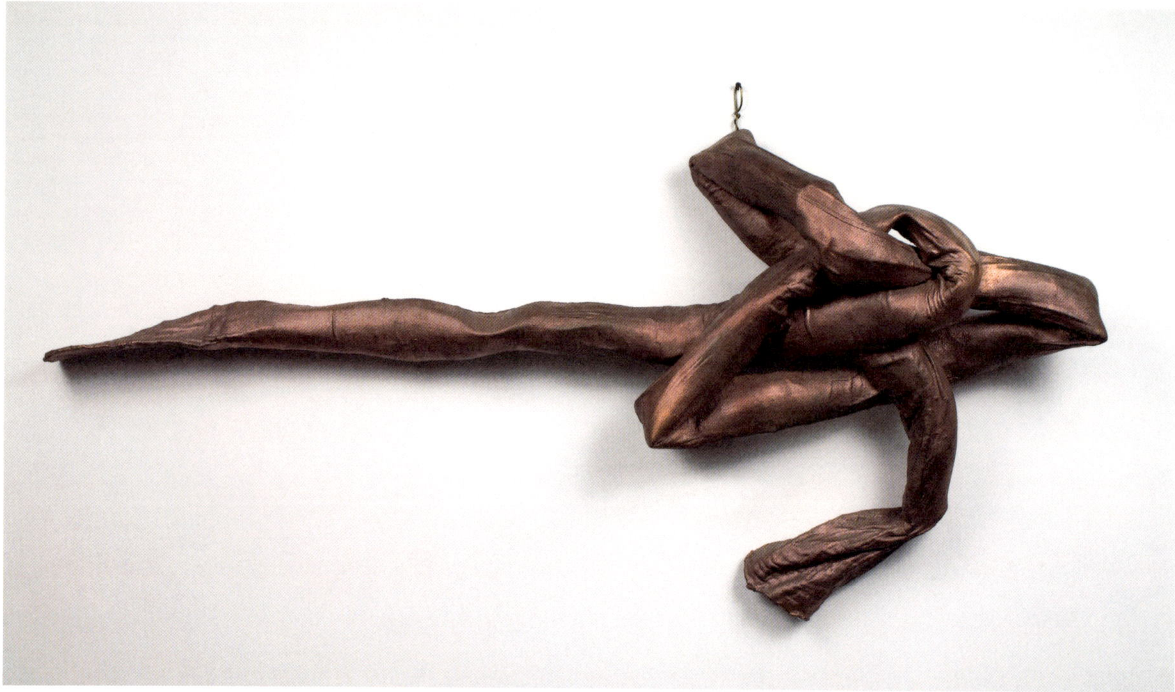

Lynda Benglis
Très (1976)
Wire mesh, cotton bunting, plaster,
sprayed aluminium, copper
61 x 152.4 x 30.5 cm

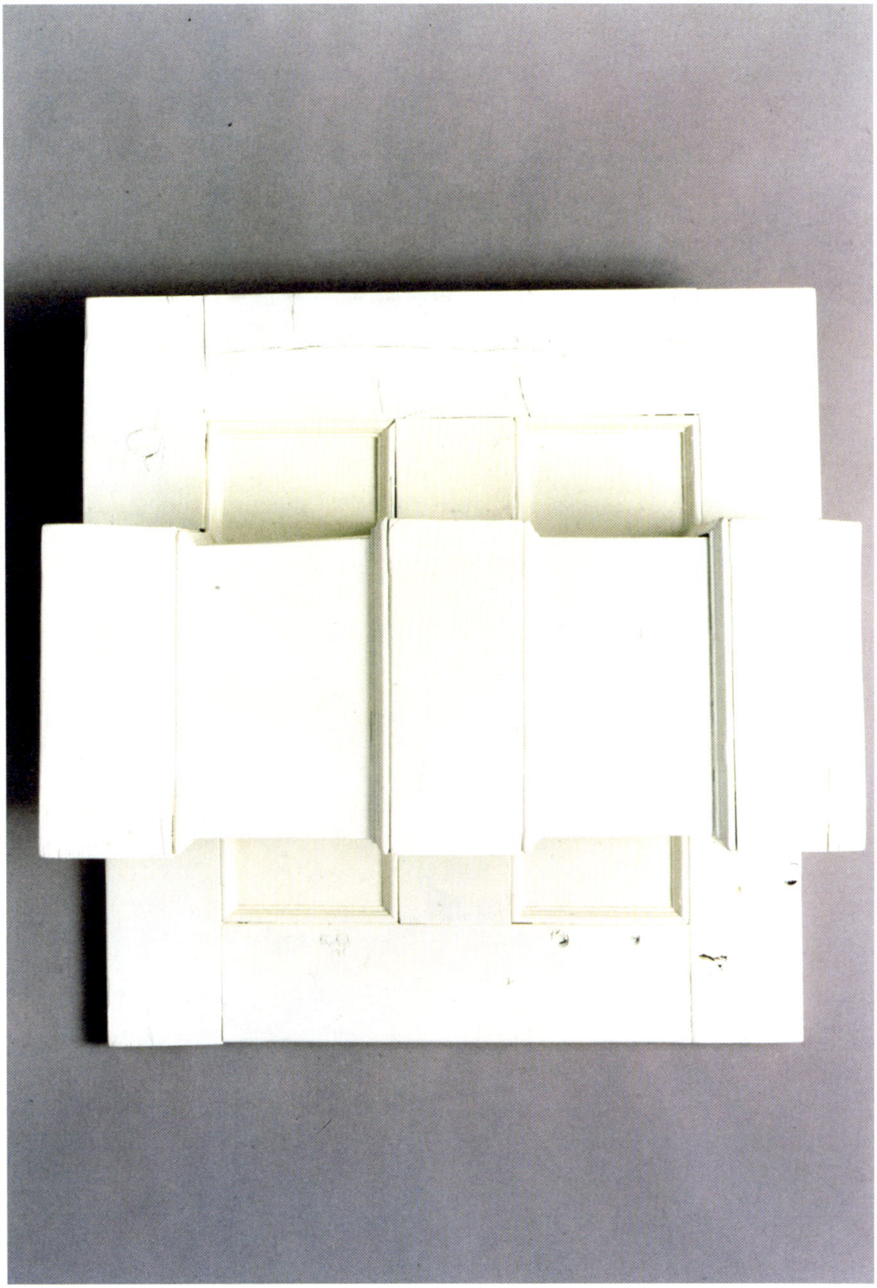

Robert Gober
Unfolding Door (1989)
Enamel on wood, steel
85 x 85 x 47 cm

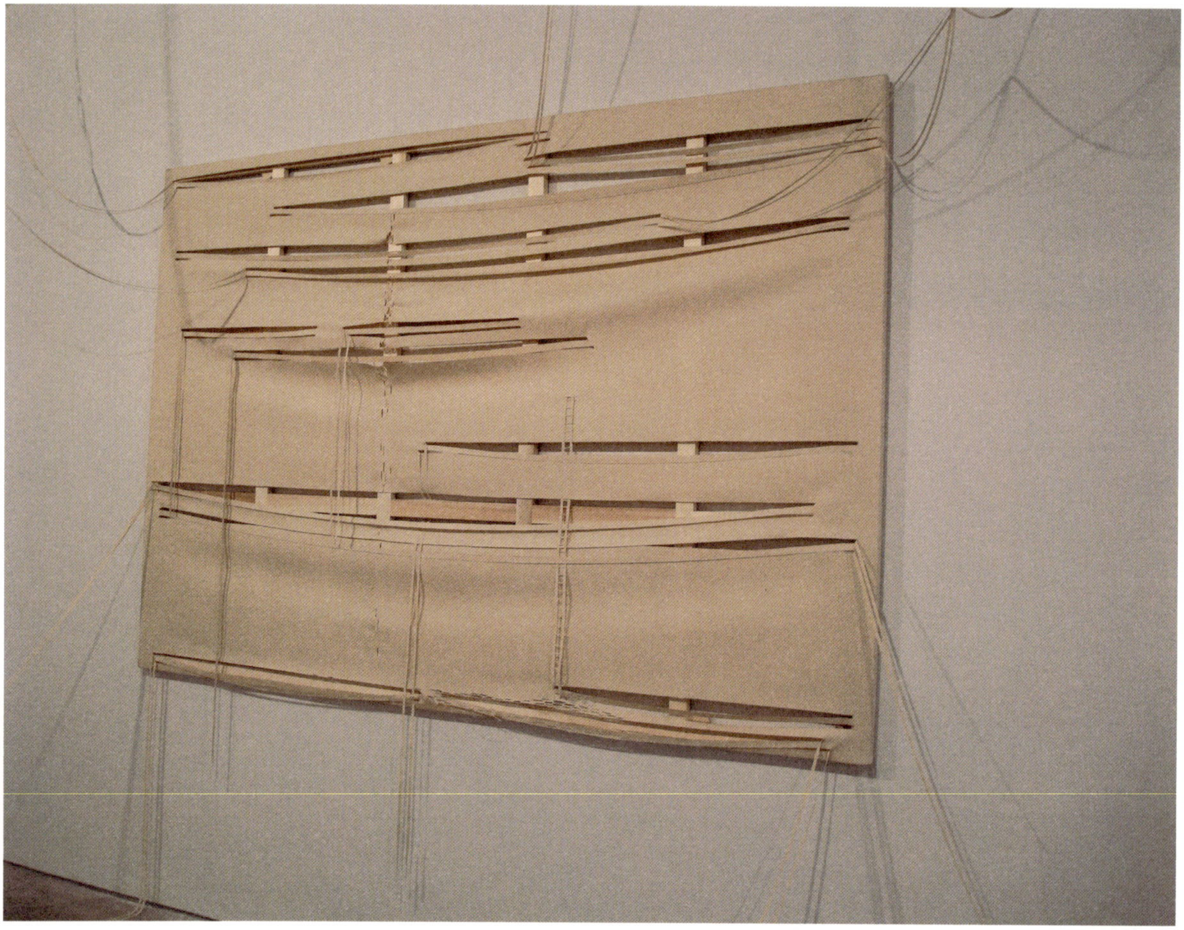

Daniel Subkoff
All Her Clothes Are Swept Aside by Her Face (2008)
Canvas
200 x 300 cm/
Dimensions variable

Kori Newkirk
Virgil (2002)
Braids, aluminium, beads, dye
166 x 122 cm

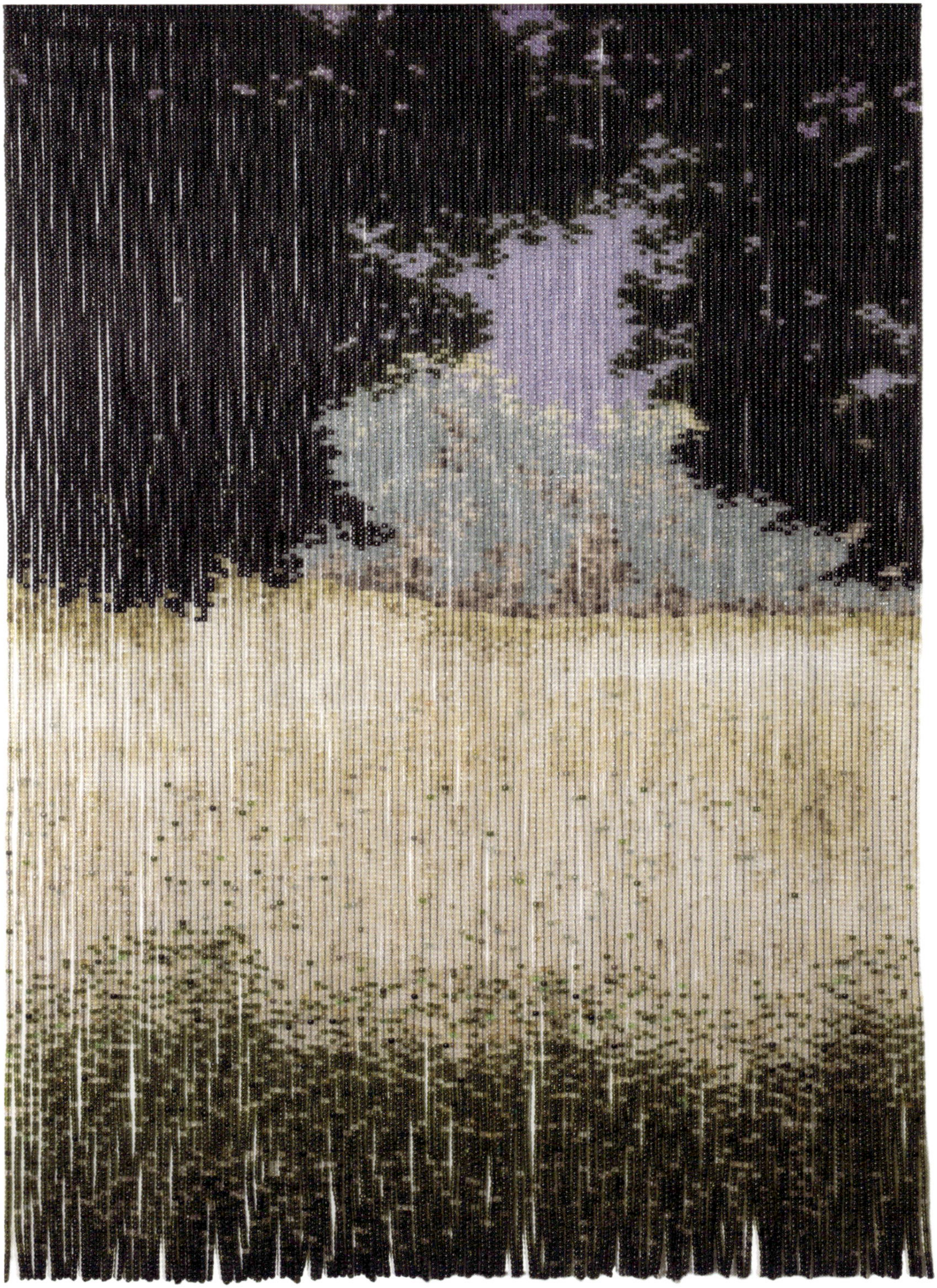

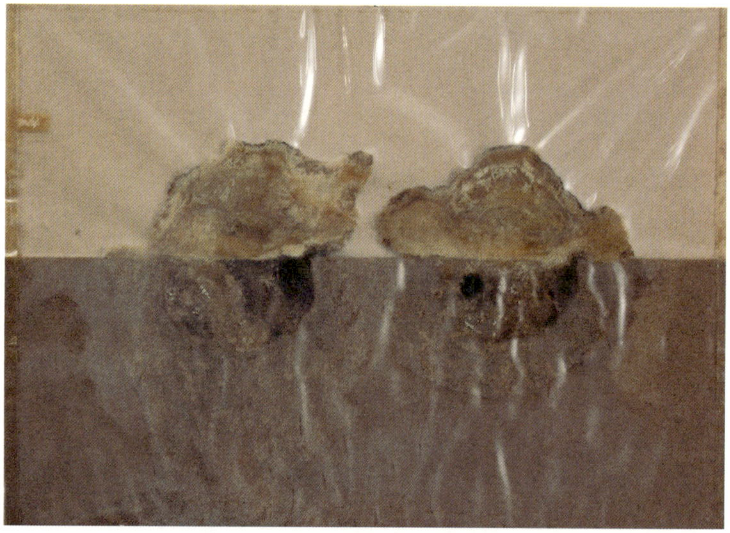

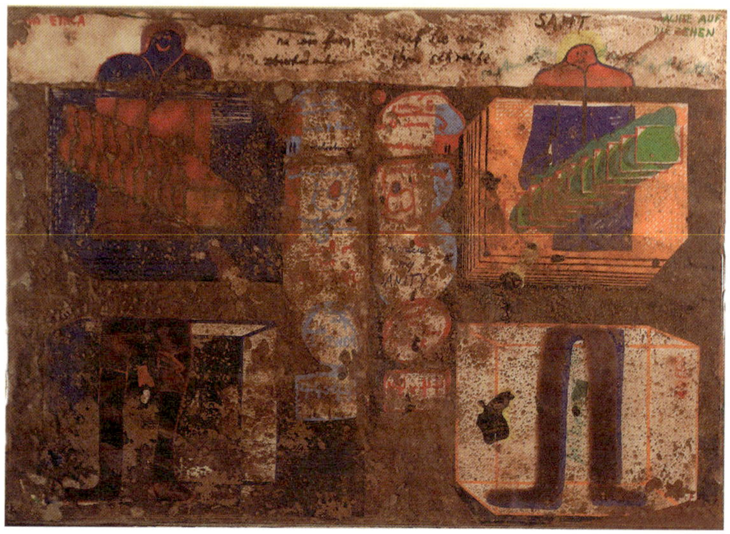

Dieter Roth

Kleine Landschaft (1969)
Cheese on sandpaper
in plastic sleeve
32 x 43.5 cm

Grafik mit Kakao (1969)
Screenprint with chocolate
in a plastic wrapper
70 x 100 cm

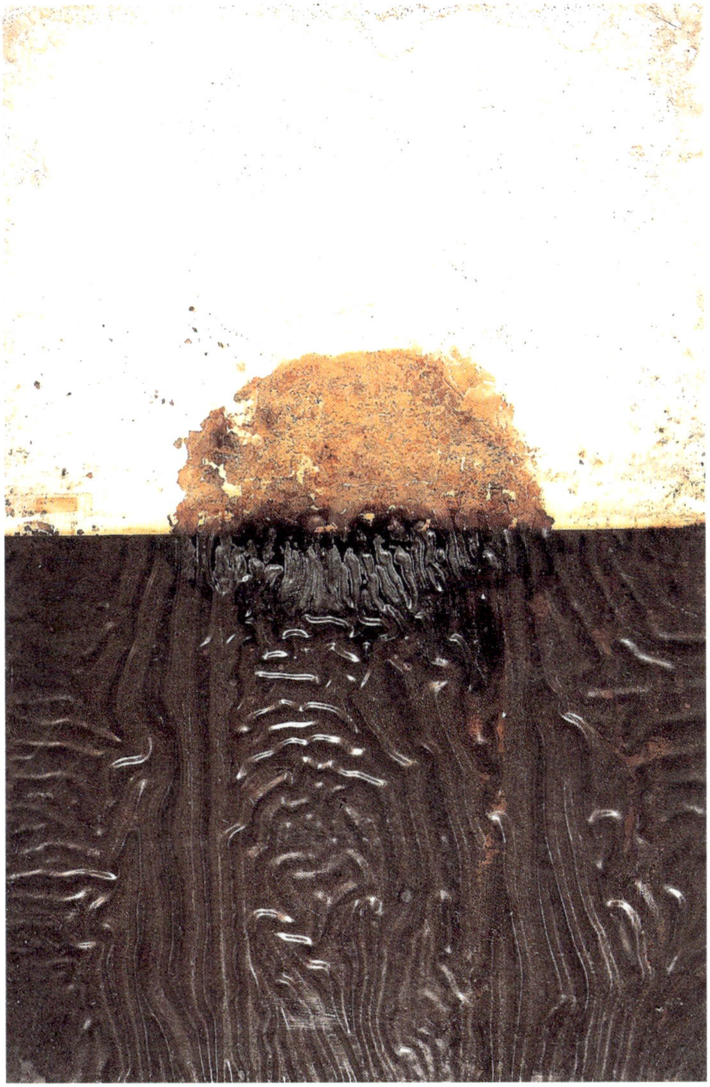

Grosse Landschaft (1969)
Pressed cheese on roofing
felt within artist's frame
98 x 65.3 cm

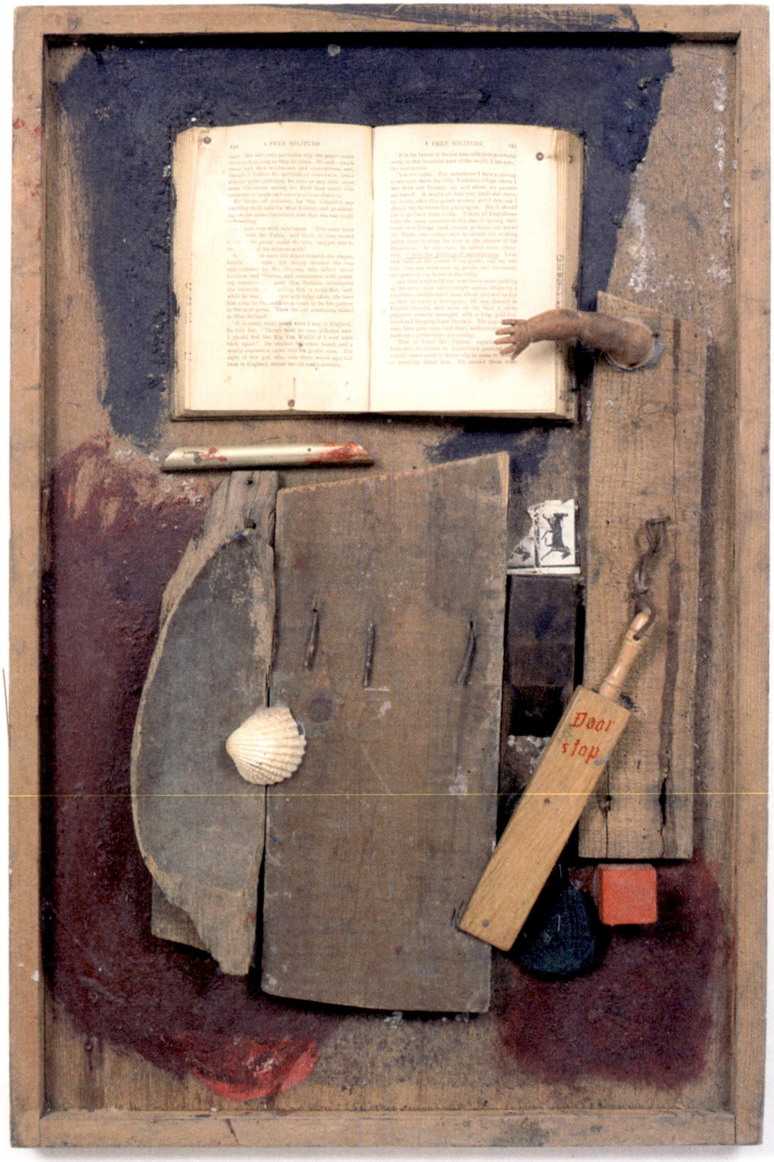

Damien Hirst
Untitled (Collage 2) (1985)
Mixed media
69 x 46 cm

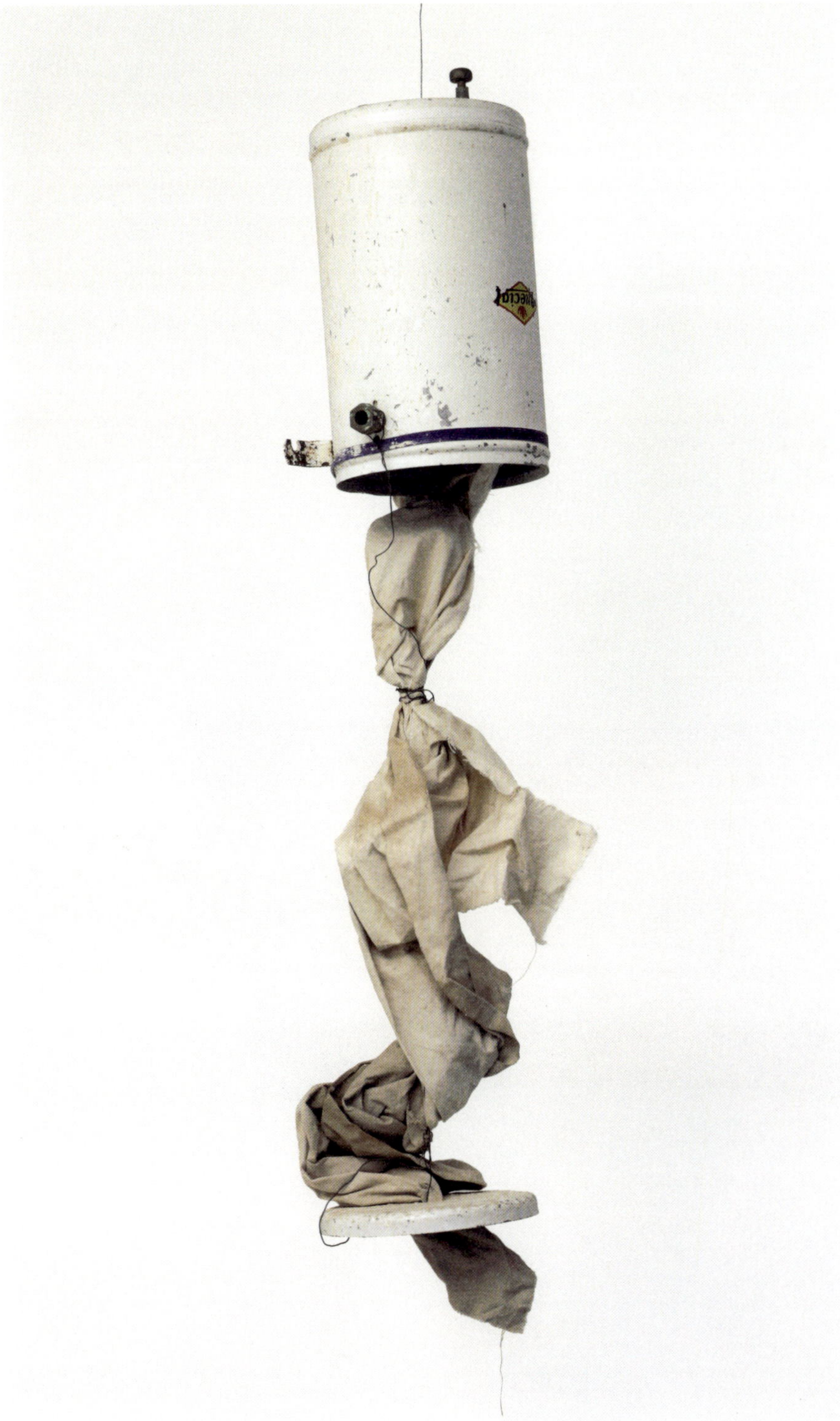

Nikos Kessanlis
Untitled (Gesture) (1961)
Ready-made object,
tissue, wire
200 x 21 cm

Mike Kelley
Transplant (1990)
Mixed media
343 x 77 cm

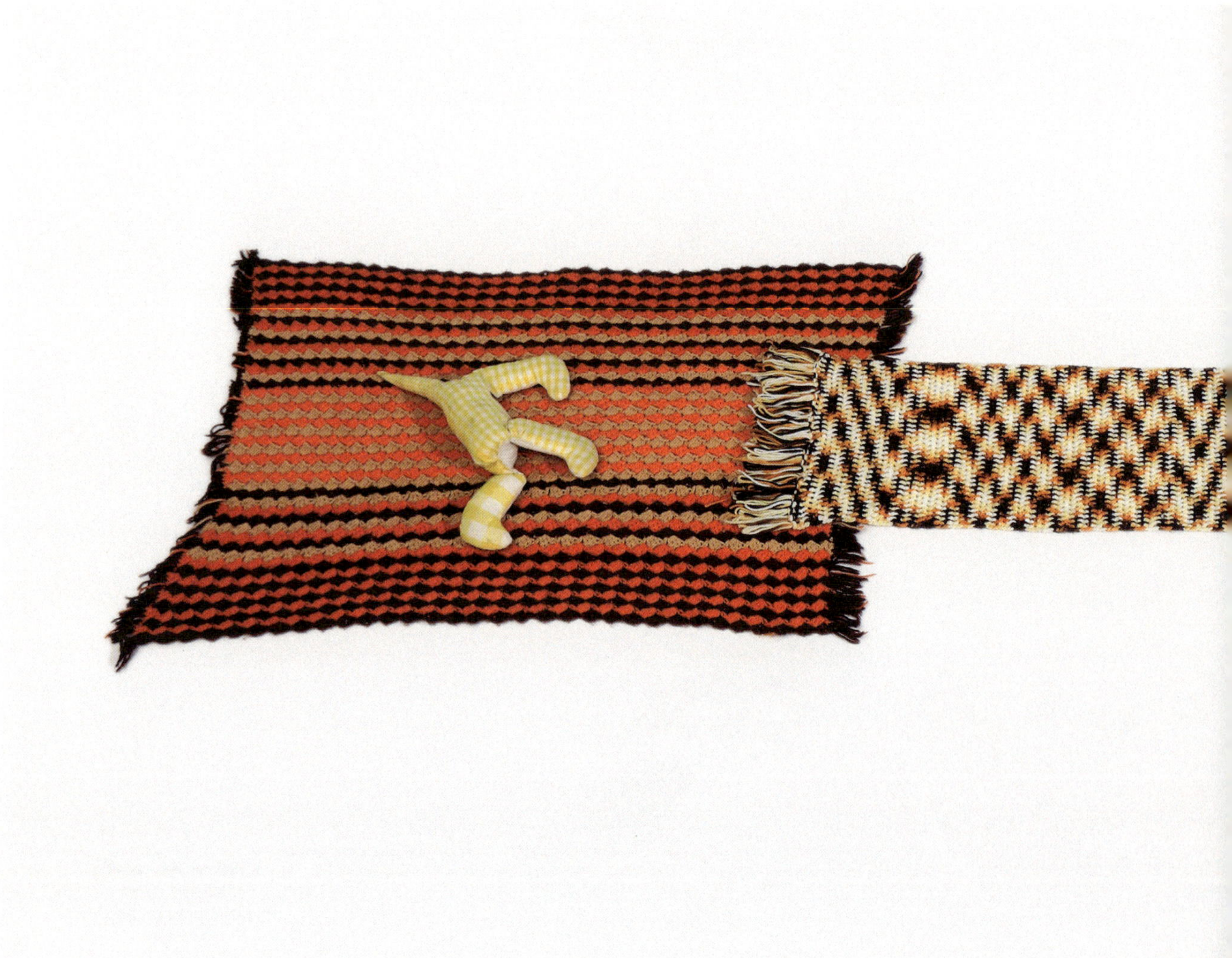

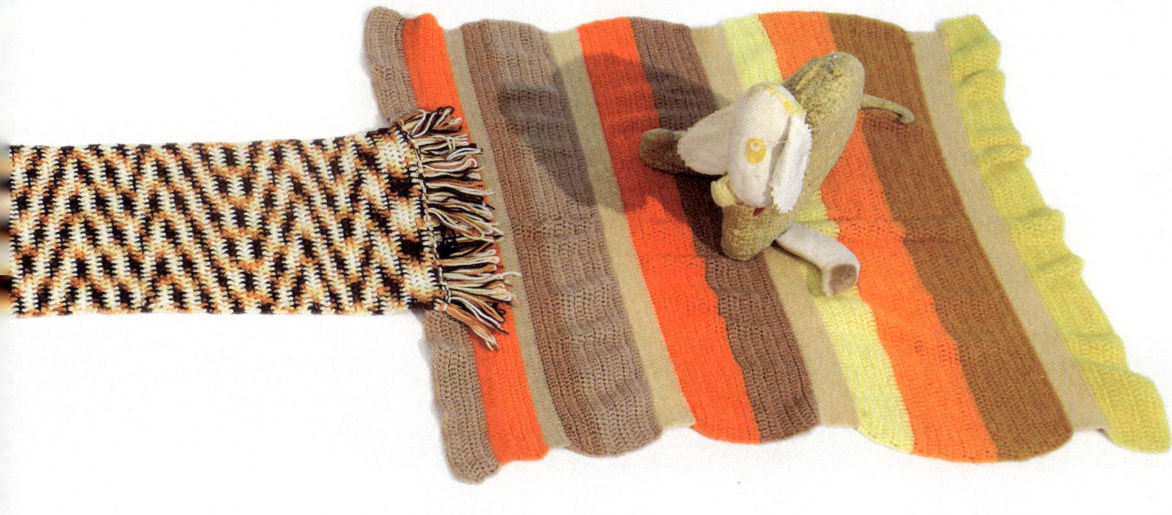

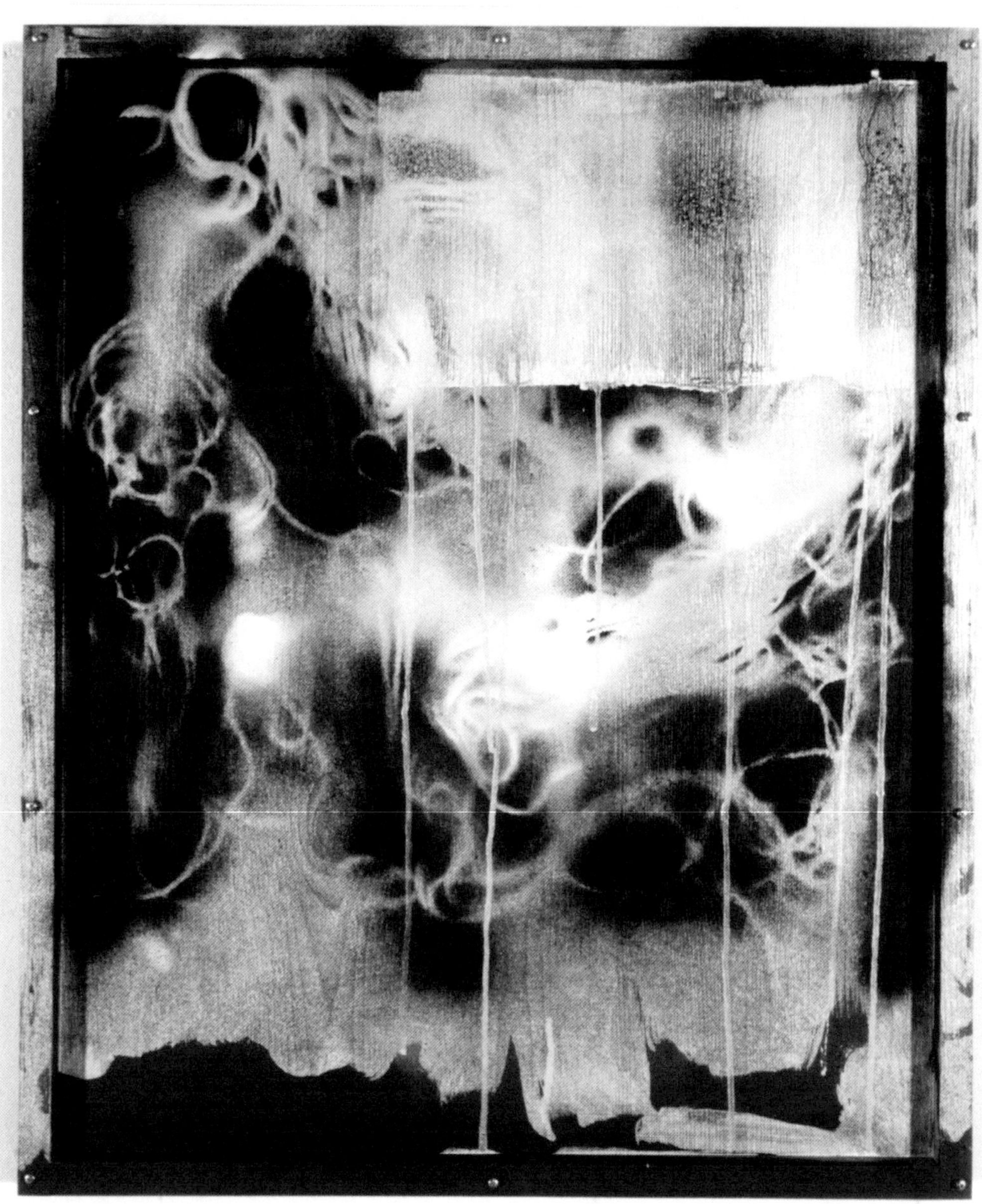

Rosemarie Trockel
Something of Tomorrow 1 (2008)
Mixed media
68 x 58 x 5 cm

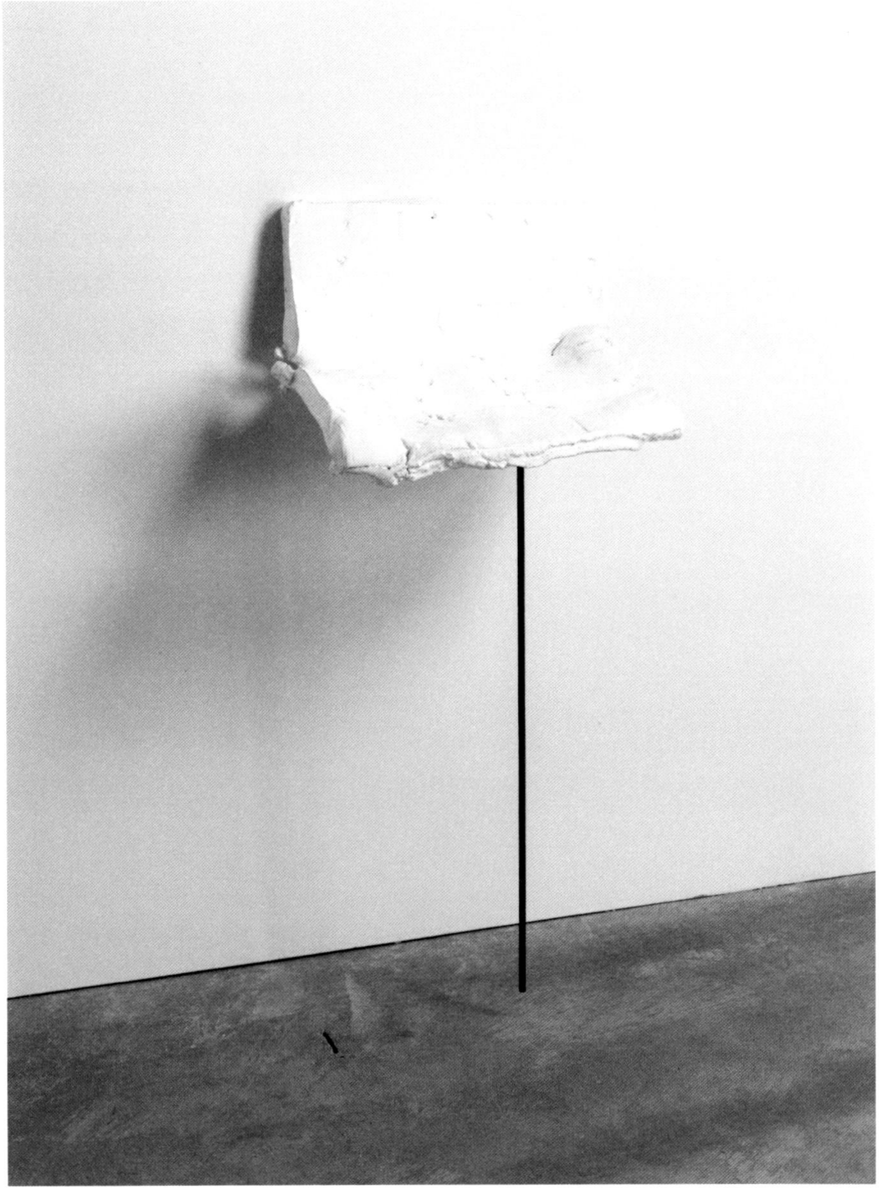

Avalanche (2008)
Glazed ceramic, metal
113 x 53 x 38 cm

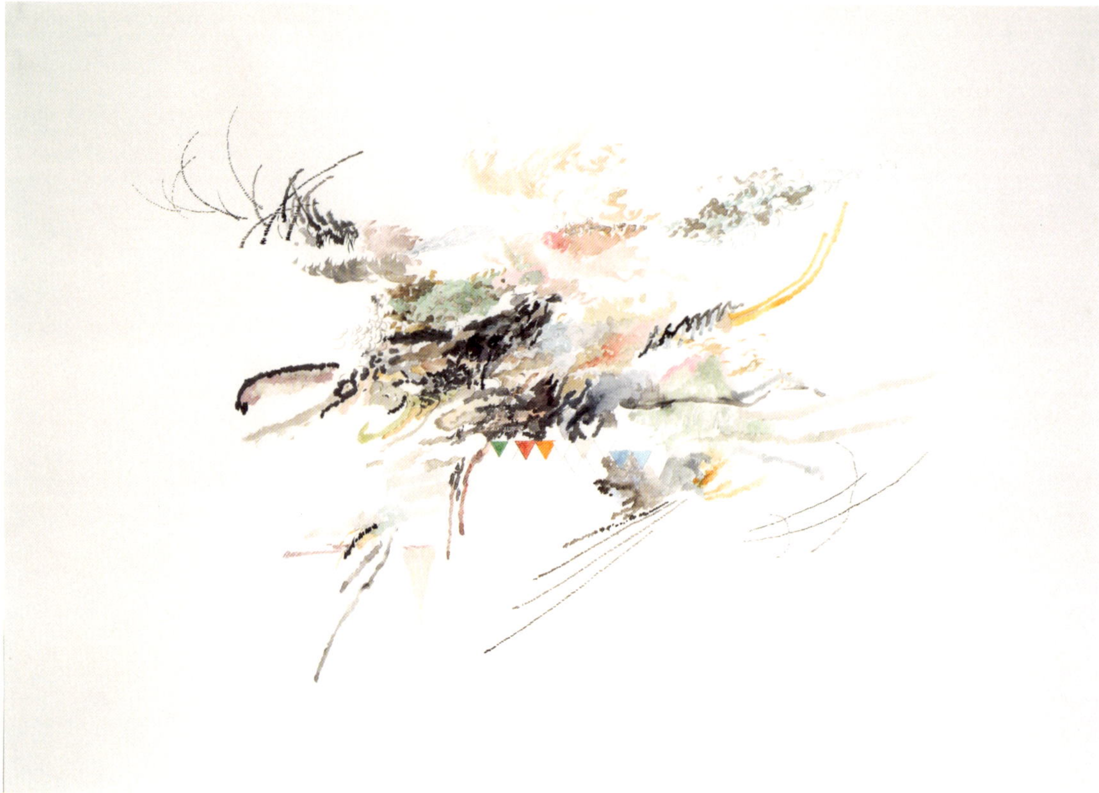

Julie Mehretu
Untitled (2006)
Graphite, ink,
watercolour on paper
71.1 x 101.6 cm

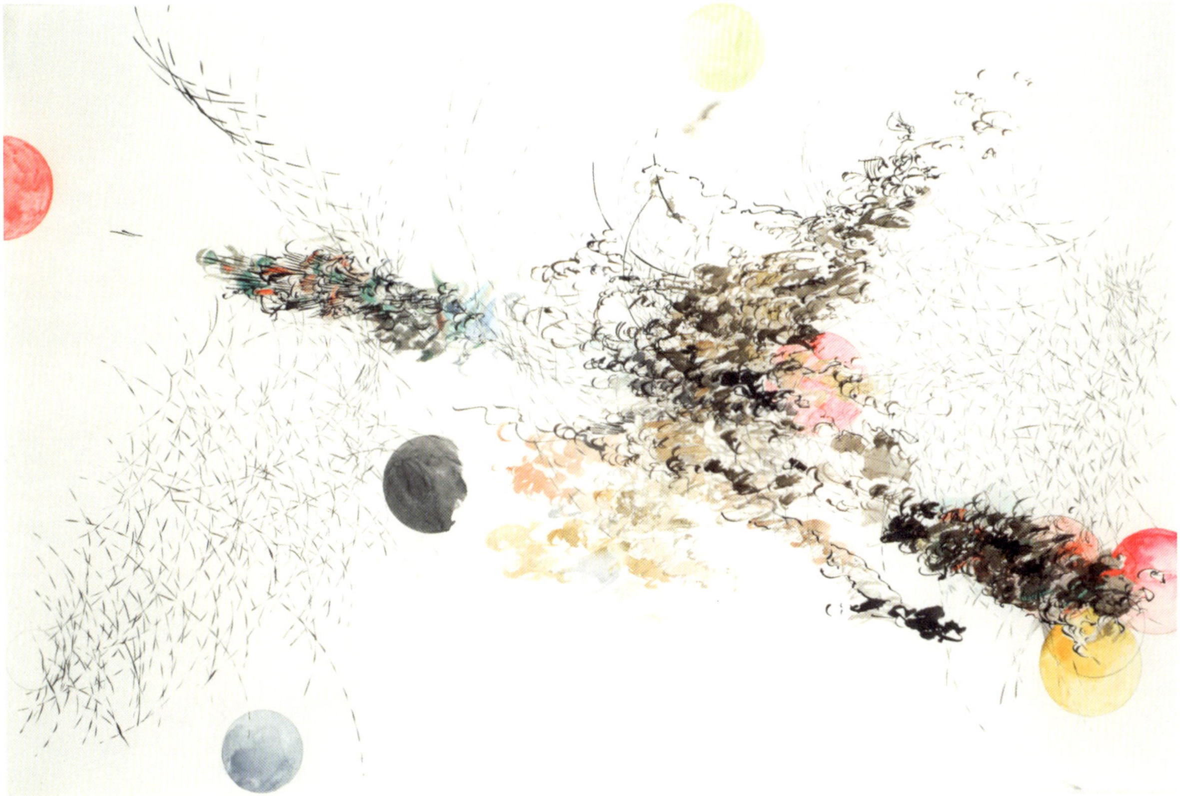

Untitled (2006)
Graphite, ink,
watercolour on paper
66 x 101.6 cm

Current Disturbance

Act

3

Current Disturbance

When I first went to England it became immediately apparent to me that people were quite divorced from their bodies and very caught up in their heads, like disembodied intellects. So I was always insisting on the physical in my work. I did not want my work to be one-dimensional in the sense that it just appeals to the intellect. I wanted it to be a complete experience that involves your body, your senses, your mind, your emotions, everything.
Mona Hatoum[1]

Mona Hatoum's works, from her early performances and videos to her sculptures and large-scale installations, are deeply rooted in the lived experience of day-to-day existence. Many draw on rendering familiar objects and materials such as household utensils strange and uncanny by changing their scale or undermining their ability to function.

Current Disturbance is a large sculptural installation consisting of 240 wire cages stacked up to form the four connecting walls of a transparent, yet impenetrable enclosure. Each cage contains a light bulb individually wired to a junction box at the centre of the structure. The bulbs light up and fade out in an irregular pattern with no clearly intelligible rationale, sporadically illuminating the surrounding room and the unruly mass of wiring covering the floor. An amplifier transforms the electric current feeding the lights into a disquieting sound track, which switches from tranquil hum to enervating crackle, and whose intensity weakens or increases as the electric current feeding the lights surges and recedes. The experience of *Current Disturbance* is intensely physical, the visual and the audible entering into a highly charged dynamic, with the viewer being given sufficient space to circumnavigate the installation, but not to adopt a distant and detached vantage point.

Both the body and systems of abstraction are equally valid points of reference in Hatoum's work. In the early 1980s, she undertook a series of performances which set up an often highly confrontational relationship with the audience. These included Hatoum confining herself to a translucent cubicle filled with slippery mud as the audience witnessed her unsuccessful attempts to achieve a stable position, or her dragging a pair of Doc Marten boots around Brixton Market. In her later sculptures and installations, the body, mostly her own, remained present through the materials deployed. Hair collected from bath plugs, combs and brushes, for instance, formed the raw material for *Recollection* (1995) while *Corps étranger* (1994), via the use of endoscopy, exposed the continuity of the body's surface, inside and out, to troubling effect.

Distrustful of overly determined messages Hatoum began in the late 1980s to draw on the formal tropes of Minimalism, such as the grid, for works whose meaning, while full of allusions to concrete social and political realities, remained purposefully open-ended. One of the earliest examples for this strategy is *The Light at the End* (1989) which deployed the glow and warmth generated by a set of heating coils to create a tense dynamic between visual attraction and physical repulsion. Rather than illustrate an idea, Hatoum forced viewers into a position where they would experience risk, danger, anxiety and fear with primeval directness.

The same applies to *Current Disturbance*. The movement of light and the spatial set up surreptitiously seduce the viewer into circulating the structure in search of an entrance. Yet, there is no point of entry. Paradoxically, while the walls of the cages shelter the viewer from the potentially harmful electric currents that fuel the light bulbs, the experience is less one of protection than of exclusion. Though outside the danger zone, being trapped between the cages and the gallery walls creates a disconcerting sense of confinement.

Current Disturbance, by virtue of its everyday materiality, combines the formal rigour of Minimalism with the evocative suggestiveness of Surrealism's 'lost object', which, encountered by chance, triggers a chain of associations that relate to subconscious fears and desires. This becomes especially apparent when one compares Hatoum's installation with Bruce Nauman's *Double Steel Cage Piece* (1974). Where Nauman's two cages with their clean lines and hard surfaces appear to have been produced industrially the simple wooden beams and wire mesh of *Current*

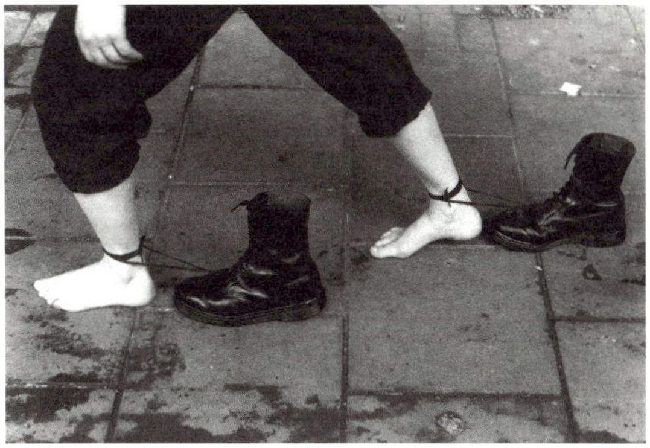

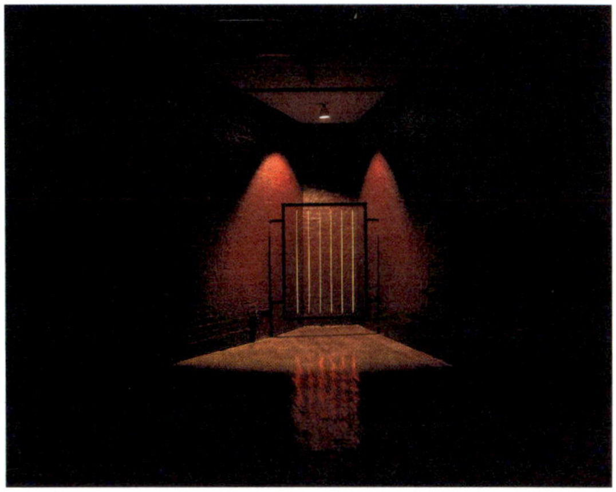

Mona Hatoum
Roadworks (1985)
Live action with
Doc Martens Boots
21 May 1985, Brixton, London

Mona Hatoum
The Light at the End (1989)
Angle iron frame, six
electric heating elements
166 x 162.5 x 5cm

Disturbance speak the universal language of entrapment from prison cells to makeshift fences or battery chicken farms. And where in Nauman's work the viewer is co-opted as performer by negotiating the tight space between the cages, set Russian-doll style inside each other, Hatoum's installation is encountered as an autonomous, self-sufficient system that the viewer cannot access, the light bulbs acting as the structure's active inhabitants instead. It is through this use of materials which appear familiar and recognisable, though we are not quite sure from where, that *Current Disturbance* exudes an air of claustrophobia, threat and isolation which goes beyond the specifics of any particular circumstance.

The tension between the rigid grid in which the cages are arranged, the rawness of the materials, the inordinate mess of the wires and the penetrating sound creates a complex interplay of emotional and intellectual responses. On first encounter, the sensory impact of *Current Disturbance* is such that it short-circuits intellectual mediation in favour of intuitive reaction. Only at second glance does the question of meaning pose itself. Hatoum rejects the traditional Western division of mind and body, which in visual culture is reflected by the separation of the all-seeing eye from the body it inhabits. The directness of address which makes Hatoum's installation so powerful reaches back to her early performances. Only that now, it is not the artist but the work itself which performs. The flashing and fading light bulbs turn *Current Disturbance* into a living organism, not unlike a nervous system, whose motions appear suspended in a fragile equilibrium between control and chaos.

Hatoum's formal vocabulary belies her long-standing preoccupation with mechanisms of surveillance and control, as much as with architectural and institutional structures whose aim is the regimentation of individuals. *Current Disturbance's* structure is reminiscent of the Panopticon, the eighteenth-century philosopher, Jeremy Bentham's, nightmarish vision for an ideal prison whose radial layout allowed for all inmates to be observed from one all-seeing vantage point. At the same time, it replicates the modular, infinitely extendable systems of high-density urban environments. When first stranded in London, following the outbreak of civil war in her native Lebanon in 1975, Hatoum was struck by the proliferation of CCTV cameras across British high streets and the way in which the modernist architecture of estates and tower blocks – what Le Corbusier had called 'Living Machines' – ensured that their inhabitants conformed to a code of behavioural norms that pandered to the demands of productivity and social coherence. *Current Disturbance*, its title as much a literal description of Hatoum's installation as a metaphorical allusion to the state of the contemporary world, is thus a powerful reminder of the fact that no part of material culture can escape the ideological connotations of value.

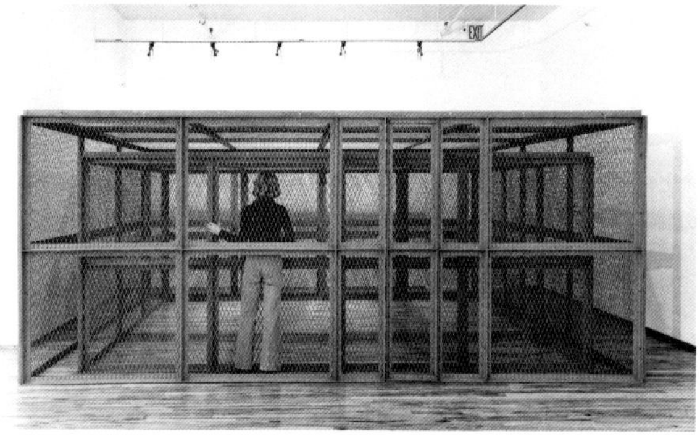

Bruce Nauman
Double Steel Cage Piece (1974)
Steel
205.9 x 392 x 520.1 cm
Collection Museum Boijmans Van Beuningen, Rotterdam

Notes

[1] Interview with Claudia Spinelli, (1996), reprinted in Michael Archer, Guy Brett, Catherine de Zegher, *Mona Hatoum* (London: Phaidon, 1997) 135.

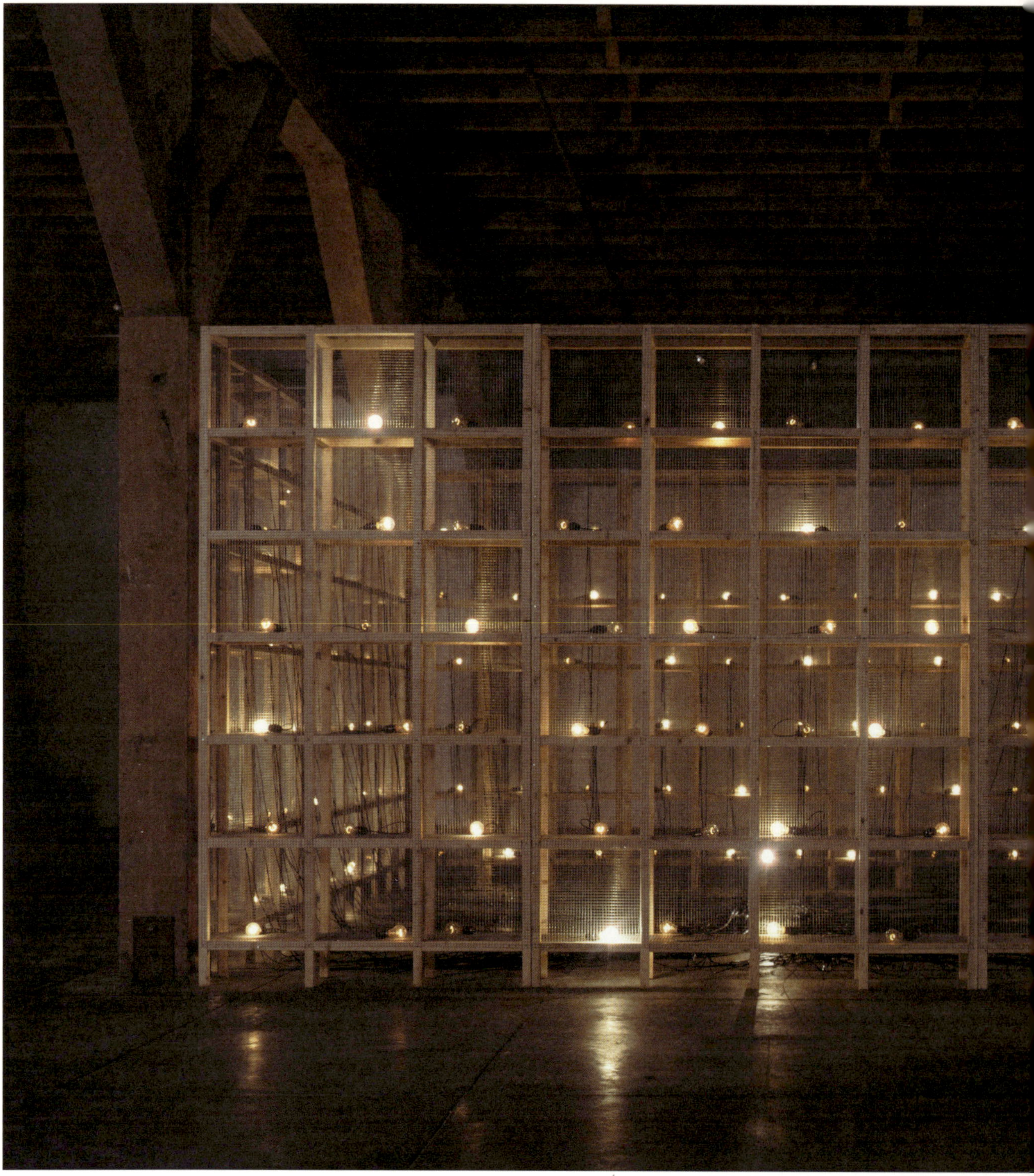

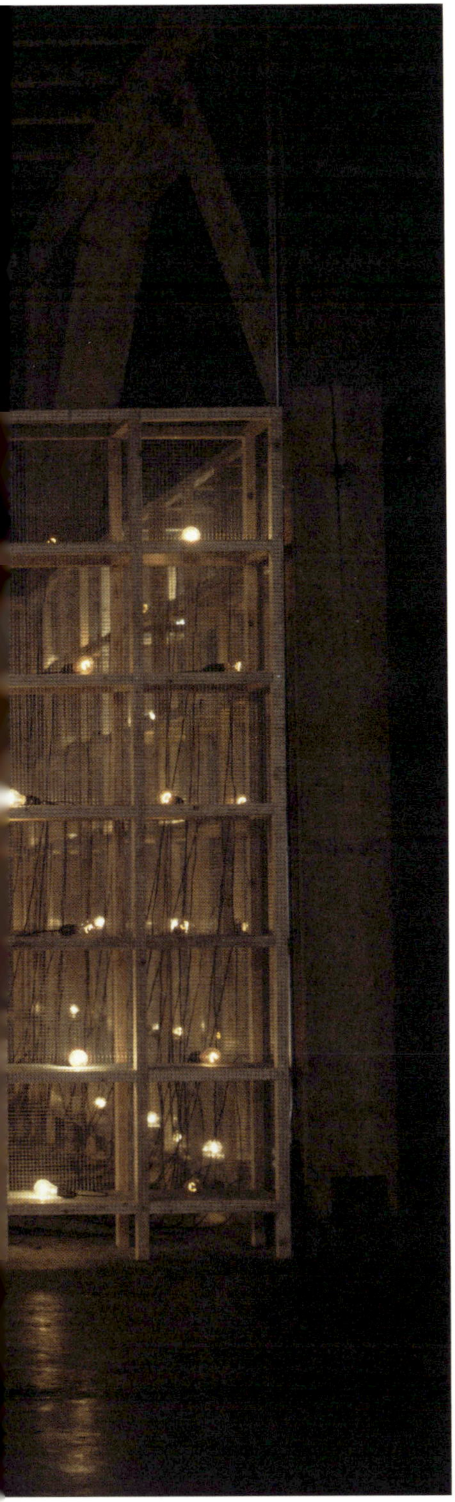

Mona Hatoum
Current Disturbance (1996)
Wood, wire mesh,
computerised dimmer
device, light bulbs
279 x 550.5 x 504 cm
Installation, Capp Street
Project, San Francisco

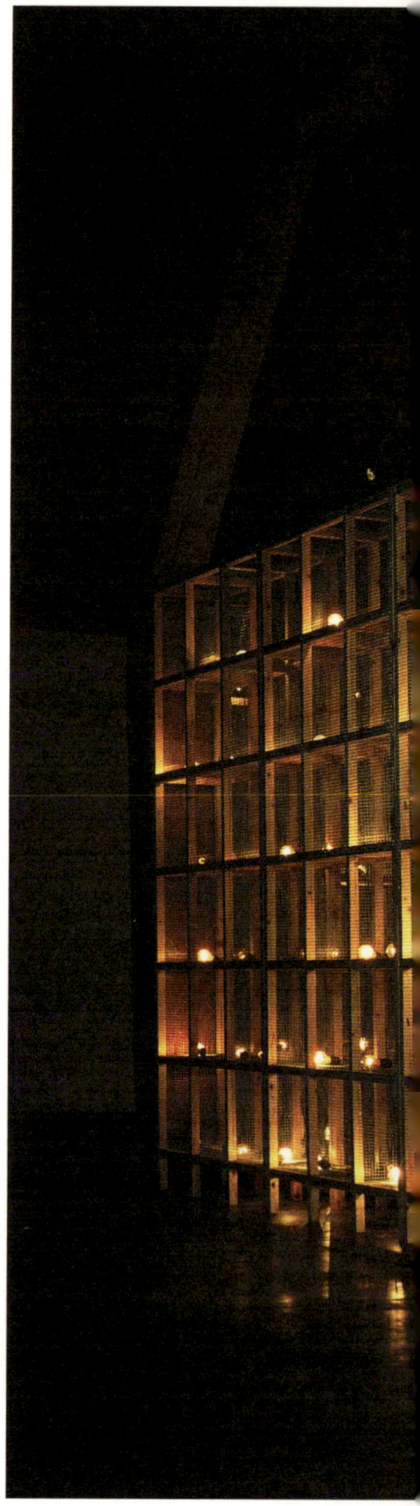

Mona Hatoum
Current Disturbance (1996)
Wood, wire mesh, computerised dimmer device, light bulbs
279 x 550.5 x 504 cm
Installation, Capp Street Project, San Francisco

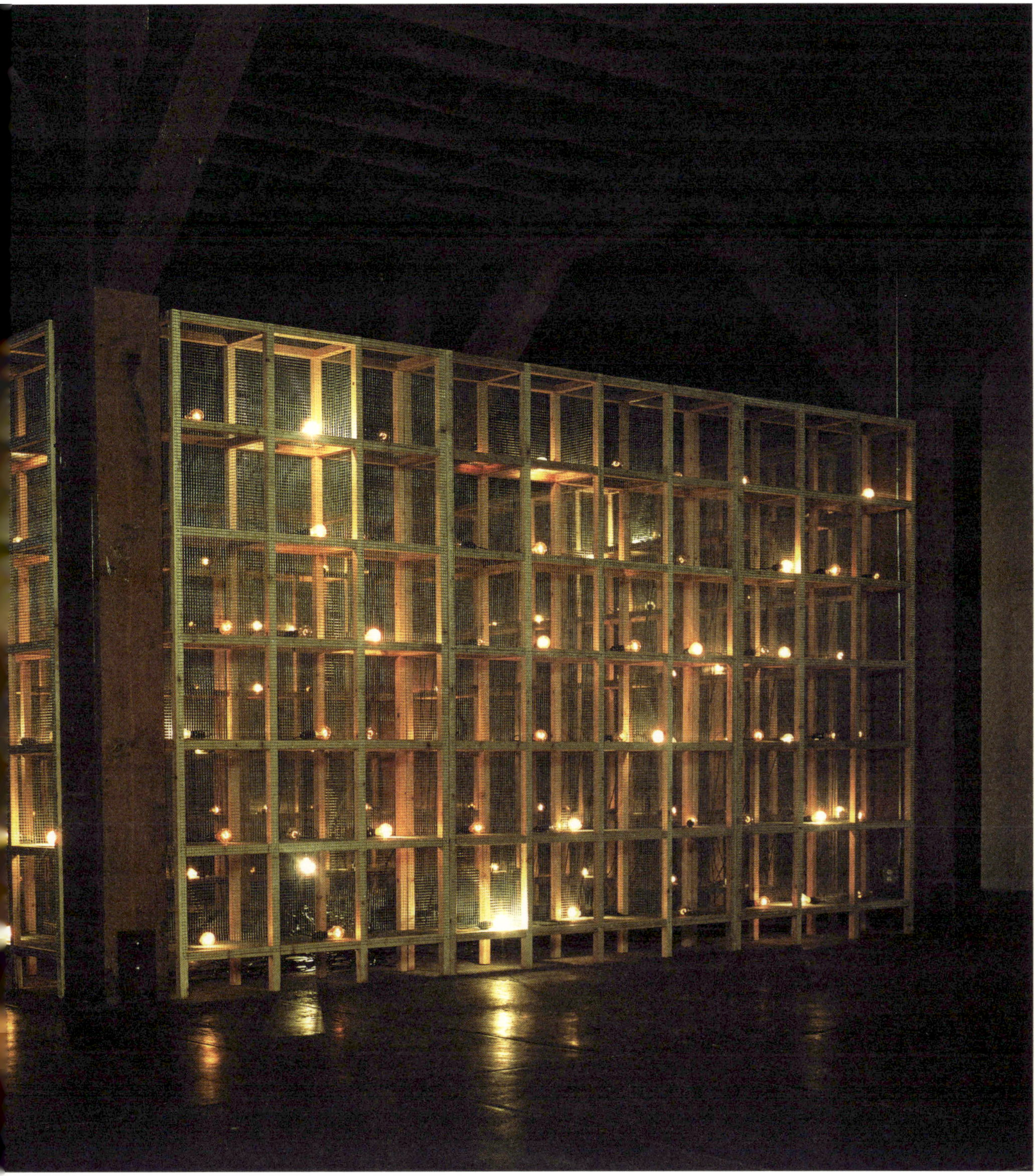

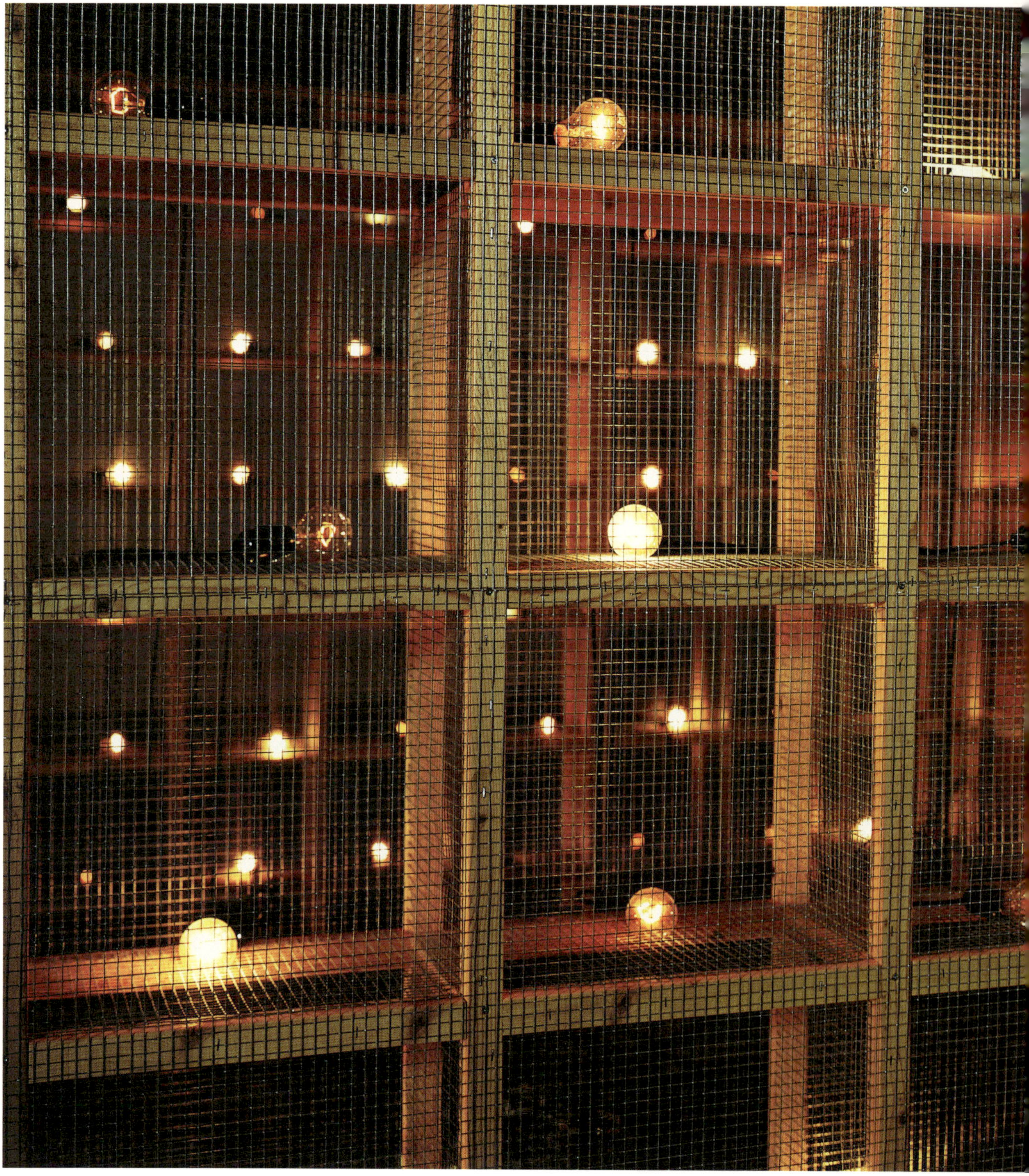

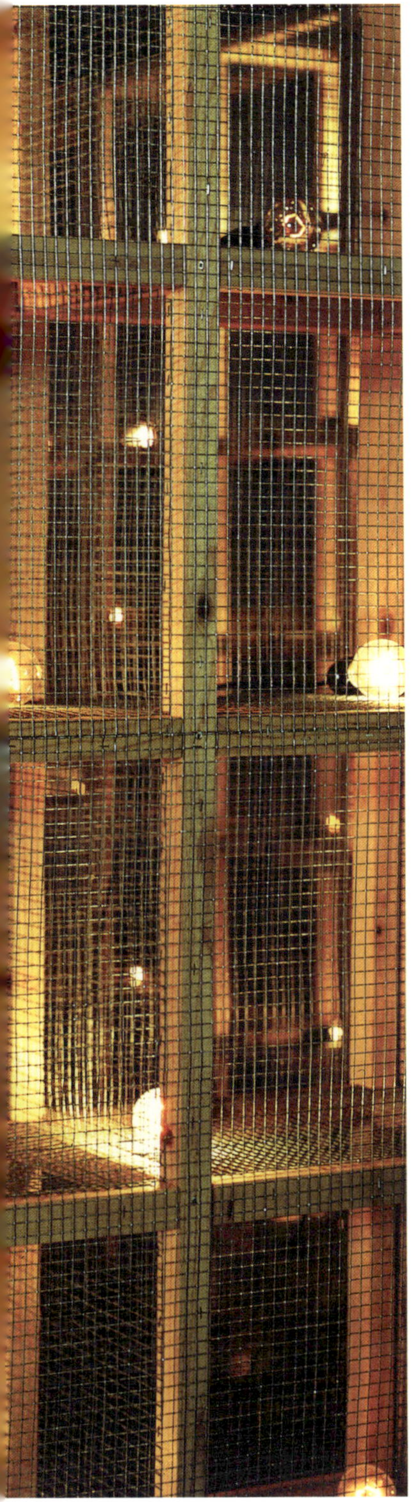

Mona Hatoum
Current Disturbance (1996)
Wood, wire mesh, computerised dimmer device, light bulbs
279 x 550.5 x 504 cm
Detail

Material Intelligence
Act 4

Material Intelligence

I try first to generate an experience for myself in what we call reality – that can be in a market or it can be with terracotta or it can even be thinking about geometry – and from that experience to generate an object that generates an experience for another person. [...] So technology and craft and the mental or the intellectual and the 'primitive' are always intersecting, and collapsing into each other.
Gabriel Orozco[1]

The modernist ideal of a universally intelligible system of thought lost further ground during the 1990s as awareness of global migration – economic, cultural and social – grew, bringing many new voices to the discourse around art. Global networks were soon balanced by a renewed preoccupation with the local, manifest in the often mundane materials artists deployed to reflect on the specifics of a particular situation. The cultural historian, Nikos Papastergiadis, observed of this phenomenon: 'Making art by taking what is close at hand. Thinking about the biggest philosophical abstractions from the position of our most intimate experiences. Seeing change as being part of our choices and responses to the inventory of demands and obligations in daily life. From this perspective, where the everyday and the dominant structures are perceived as interconnected, we can also see that art, theory and politics are in constant dialogue. One cannot proceed without the other.'[2]

The path for this new interconnectedness was paved by the growth of the media and the accelerated dissemination of information and images. Some seventy years earlier, the journalist and writer, Siegfried Kracauer had noted that: 'In the illustrated magazines, people see the very world that the illustrated magazines prevent them from perceiving'.[3] However, rather than treating the image as ideologically suspect, the end of the century saw a growing interest in the image as 'material', as yet another type of ready-made. This change in attitude, and its concomitant refusal of the image as being limited to 'virtual' reality, is evidenced not least in the various manoeuvres such as cropping, distorting and layering, which artists deployed to heighten the image's physicality.

Collage became a favourite strategy not to construct absurd and disturbing narratives as the Surrealists had done but rather to draw attention to the inherent qualities of the images used – their material support, mode of reproduction, method of construction, use of colour, etc.

This led, on the one hand, to an unprejudiced use of new technologies such as scanners, computer software and inkjet printers, and on the other, to the deployment of even the most worthless, readily available and quite unremarkable materials. As a result, the art object was pushed to the very limits of its recognisability in a way that even Duchamp would have found hard to anticipate. Flirtation with the banal often acted as self-conscious counterpoise to the loftier aspirations of earlier generations of artists. However, by no means did this equal a de-politicisation or abandonment of all earlier ideals. As Arturo Herrera observed: 'Modernism was utterly obstinate about itself. While proclaiming a world full of uncertainty, it strove toward innovation while respecting tradition. It had a visual language born of intuition with an optimistic yearning to become universal. Well, it didn't work out as planned, but the debris is endlessly complex and fertile.'[4]

Many artists began to utilise everyday materials to breathe new life into the modernist drive towards the convergence of art and life. However, they did so no longer in search of a Utopian world order but to provide critical reflection on the world as it is. In the words of media historian, Ben Highmore: 'If everyday life, for the most part, goes by unnoticed (even as it is being revolutionised), then the first task for attending to it will be to make it noticeable. [...] to register the everyday in "all" its complexities and contradiction'.[5]

Cady Noland, for instance, draws on media images and the coincidental and messy world of vernacular objects to expose the schizophrenia and psychic disturbances that form the undercurrent of US popular culture. 'I try sometimes to construct a mirror of the weird stuff that doesn't fit together, floating in a sea of palliative Gestalt images. People are able to live with the scattered and fragmented stuff because they are always reassured by the concept or the image of things that are whole.'[6] The American flag, around which people gather in a gesture of national unity that is constantly contradicted by the divisions which tear at the fabric of US society, is a prime example of this false desire for wholeness directed at an image. The banner, wrapped up and packed away, is prominently placed across a Zimmer frame in *Objectification Process* (1989), a wry commentary on the dysfunctional nature of consumerism.

Conscious of her position as a woman, Noland has a keen eye for the undiminished persuasiveness of male stereotypes in popular imagery, such as the romantic cliché of the lonesome cowboy. This goes hand-in-hand with Noland's preoccupation with social violence, which, having lost its positive potential for collective revolutionary action, is now channelled via dysfunctional individuals to uphold the status quo (Noland holds a particular fascination with the notion of the psychopath). The cut-out figure of *Cowboy Eating, with Holes and Scarf in Crotch Hole* (1990) is punctured by a series of holes that suggest its use for target practice, hitting the male where it hurts most. At the same time, Noland's use of the disc or circle recalls the way this has been used – from Wassily Kandinsky's early abstract paintings to the photo-conceptual works of John Baldessari – as a formal device to guide the viewer's eye across the picture's surface and to prevent it from coming to a standstill.

The disc motif and cut-out images also feature prominently in *Pop Art Calendar* (1991) by Martin Kippenberger, who died prematurely in 1997 at the age of 44. Operating in a context that was dominated by the re-working of German history, especially through painting, Kippenberger stood out for his attitude of ironic detachment, knowing self-stylisation as *enfant terrible*, and his refusal of accepted value hierarchies, such as the ones between good and bad taste, high art and popular culture. *Pop Art Calendar* consists of 12 collages spliced together from colour reproductions of iconic works by Pop artists including Peter Blake, Richard Hamilton, David Hockney, Robert Indiana and Roy

Lichtenstein and the identical black-and-white photograph from a nudist magazine. The colour reproductions are taken from a calendar originally produced by Deutsche Bank for its corporate clients, a witty comment on the inflationary currency of the image in the age of mass reproduction vis-à-vis the commodity status of the original work of art.

Kippenberger deployed painting as just another form of image-making, denying the medium any special status above other types of visual culture. *I Am Too Political* (1995) is made up from individual panels, each of which varies in texture and background composition, thus preventing a unified whole. The figure of an obese woman lampoons the century-long tradition of the idealised female nude. Kippenberger's proclivity for pun and punch lines is reflected by his play on the Greek words *poli, tical* and *popo*. The latter is a verbal exclamation (rather than a written word) widely used both to confer a sense of surprise and to describe a bottom in child-friendly language. The idea of politics in the sense of ideology or party-action is ridiculed here as a children's game for adults.

The ease with which images can be reproduced, manipulated and circulated, over the past decade, has become as much the subject of critical enquiry as an opener for new creative possibilities, without the former necessarily excluding the latter. In *Untitled* (2008), Kelley Walker takes the idea of the image as being constructed to its logical conclusion by literalising the subject matter – ordinary building bricks – and laying bare the physical build-up of the image surface (silk-screen print on newspaper mounted onto canvas). To do so, Kelley purposefully chooses the formal conventions of painting, the arena most loaded ideologically to explore the translation of an already existing image – even if nowhere else other than in the mind of the artist – into an art object. It is not just the motif of ordinary bricks which connects *Untitled* to the everyday, but also the use of readily available new technologies including computer scanning and Photoshop, all of which have become part of daily life. Kelley uses these in a consciously throw-away manner, scratching the flatbed scanner as he places heavy bricks directly onto its surface or drags it around buildings to scan sections of existing walls.

The nature of the image is explored further through the overlaying of disparate visual information and by offsetting the ephemeral nature of media imagery – the newspaper which serves as ground – against the endurance of the work of art and the stasis of the brickwork. The importance of time, and how this frames our relationship to images, is highlighted by Kelley mounting a complete edition of the newspaper, which the title identifies as the 28 January 2008 edition of the French broadsheet *Le Figaro*, on the back of the canvas. Accessible only to the work's owner or specialist technicians, this is a hidden time capsule that, not unlike On Kawara's date paintings, expressly ties the work to its temporal context.

In contrast, Seth Price's *Untitled (Whispering, Feeding)* (2008) withholds precisely the visual information that is needed to unlock its meaning. Recycling digital images pulled from unidentified sources, Price has produced two complex black and red laser-cut shapes. It is only by virtue of our brain's ceaseless search for identifiable imagery that, similar to an old-fashioned vexation game, we read these shapes as the space 'between' various human interactions such as confiding a secret or providing nourishment. This manoeuvre results in a paradoxical sense of delight at having deciphered the visual clues given when effectively the information provided is insufficient to develop a specific narrative. Hence, our reading of the shapes becomes as generic as the images on whose familiarity it is reliant. Prime among these are moving images and the conventions of cinematic gestures.

The latter also serve as starting point for Paul Chan's work. His richly textured grisaille collages are closely connected to his video projections, especially his series of *Lights* (2005–7). Chan has pointed out that despite the omnipresence of the moving image, not least within the context of art, its framework has remained relatively unchanged: a sharply defined field with the projected images acting as a window for the imagination (the way painting had done in

Kelley Walker
Untitled (2008)
Four-colour process silkscreen on canvas with collage of *Le Figaro*, Monday 28 January 2008
121.9 x 243.8 cm
Detail of reverse view

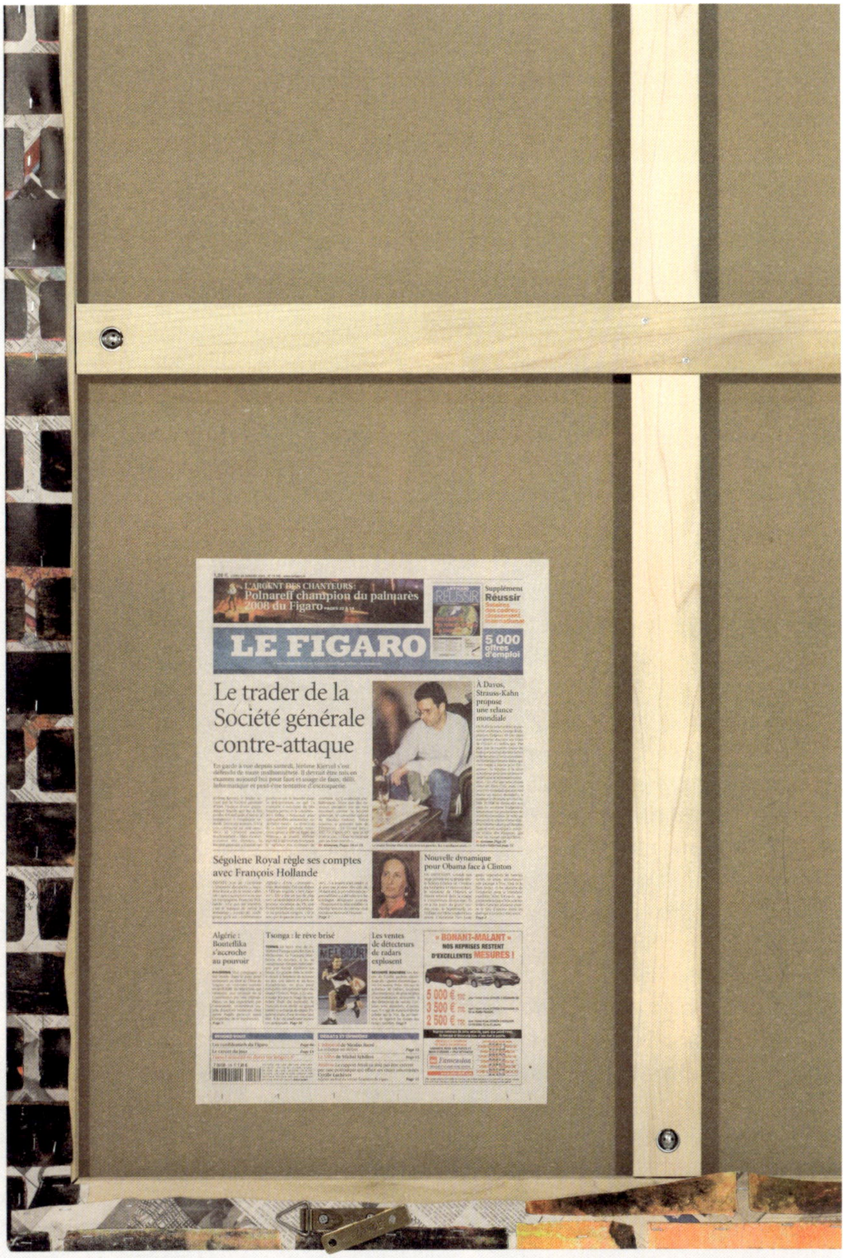

the past). Moving image technology relies on the contrast of light and darkness which carries loaded cultural connotations. According to the Platonic view of the world, all we ever see is the shadow of things with their ontological essence hidden from view (not by darkness, but by light). The shadow was also used to great effect by Marcel Duchamp in the photographic images he took of his ready-mades (or their shadows, to be more precise).[7] Chan has observed of his work that: 'Everyone feels that art, as a historical bookmark for an ideality of something, could, in and of itself, be the symbol that it longs to be. Which is to say, something exchangeable for all. And so the task was to treat it like something else.'[8] The black shapes in Chan's collages give no clue as to the nature of the objects that cast their shadows, creating a sense of unease only heightened by the instability of their formal arrangement.

A similar play between recognisable forms and disorientating abstraction also informs the work of Arturo Herrera. Vernacular images such as those from comic strips, cartoons and advertising have arguably become far more universal than the purist visual language proposed by the early Modernists. Travelling at great speed across different cultural contexts, they are signifiers for global connectivity as much as for the sense of estrangement that characterises the 'unplace' of the contemporary condition where individual identity can no longer be located in a single place. At the same time, Herrera's collages, by combining fragments of his own canvases with found materials speculate on the challenges for the artist – and especially the painter – to create new coherent images in an environment that is already over-saturated with visual referents of all kinds.

Though Sam Durant's work also contains complex chains of reference, both historical and art-specific, his use of materials generates a surprisingly immediate encounter. The title of his *La Plus Belle Sculpture* (2007) quotes a popular slogan from the 1968 Paris uprisings: 'The most beautiful sculpture is a paving stone thrown into the face of a police man'. The words are graffitied twice – once from left to right, once in reverse – onto a mirror. Blobs of spray paint suggest a violent attack. Mirrors were widely used by many artists working in the late 1960s including Dan Graham, Joan Jonas, Robert Morris, Bruce Nauman, Michelangelo Pistoletto and Robert Smithson. Despite differences in approach, many of them shared a certain scepticism towards the dominant social and political power structures, which was reflected in the often 'poor', non-art materials they deployed. For many who grew up in the 1960s, such as Durant, this period is shrouded in the myth of marking the end of authentic political activism. His work, which is as playful as it is serious, balances nostalgia for the attainability of utopian ideals of the past with a de-masking of the dystopian reality these frequently result in.

Ester Partegàs focuses on consumption as one defining aspect of contemporary reality. She is especially interested in the way in which consumer goods and brands convey descriptive information about the people who use them. *It's an Individual Experience (We the People)* (2006) plays on the dilemma of being torn between an excessive emphasis on individualisation and a yearning for communality. Striving to assert what makes us 'us', we fall back on mass-produced articles that are inherently antithetical to gaining a true sense of self. Here, the faces of the crowd crossing the city are erased by spray paint and the collaged title, so that the shopping bags take on a heightened importance as hallmarks of personal identity.

The work of Gabriel Kuri, similar to that of Durant and Partegàs, also mobilises the dynamic between materials and semantics, though in his they often cancel each other out. The title of *Quick Standards* (2006) plays on the latter's double-meaning: the abstract concept of measure, parameter, pattern and paradigm, on the one hand; and the concrete object of banner or political tool, on the other. It also alludes to Duchamp's early ready-made, *3 Standard Stoppages* (1913–14), a glib pun on accepted norms.[9] Kuri's standards are made from metal foil emergency blankets, designed to prevent heat loss in harmed bodies; however, their blank, reflective surfaces are void of any directional message. Using cheap materials and a minimum of intervention, Kuri's work updates the ready-made's question of what distinguishes the art object from any other object, and in what way it functions differently. Reflecting on the notion of value, Kuri has observed that: 'My work is about having a critical viewpoint on the act of making.'[10]

Lightness of touch and attention to the ordinarily overlooked stuff of daily life are also central to the work of Gabriel Orozco: 'I do believe that a work you do in five seconds can be as strong as a work you do in one year's time, so I believe in small-gesture potential'.[11] The latter was famously borne out at the 1993 Venice Biennale when Orozco exhibited an empty shoe box which was barely noticeable. Removing the institutional tropes Duchamp's original ready-mades had relied on, Orozco pushes the conflation of art and reality even further, often turning the viewer from passive bystander into active participant. *Moon Tree* (1996), one of eight similar trees, originally lined a set of bowling lanes, made from pin-striped suit cloth, which formed part of a large-scale interactive installation commissioned for an empty gentlemen's club in London's St James' area. Each of the trees' leaves is intersected by a circular disc, a motif Orozco regularly employs to activate the process of perception. Here they also make a link to the 'moon' of the title, connecting the most insignificant of material interventions with an engagement with the world that expands out into the cosmos. Orozco's poetic manoeuvre imbues the ready-made with a transformative potential that further blurs the lines between art and reality: 'What is most important is not so much what people see in the gallery or the museum, but what people see after looking at these things, how they confront reality again.'[12]

Rivane Neuenschwander describes her use of ephemeral materials lifted from everyday life as 'ethereal materialism'.[13] *Contingent* (2008) shows a swarm of ants devouring a map of the world rendered in honey, their hearty appetite turned into comical terror via the use of time-lapse photography. Eating, and the notions of ingesting and digesting, are recurring motifs in Neuenschwander's work. *Antropofógia*, or cannibalism, in Brazilian modernist discourse was used as metaphor for the country's ability to absorb external influences rather than to succumb to them. Psychoanalytic theory links *antropofógia* with the melancholic's disposition to 'swallow' the object of his loss.[14] Rather than the construction of an image, Neuenschwander's film shows the most universally recognisable image, the world, disappearing in front of our eyes, a wry comment perhaps that in the age of globalisation the question of survival (and of a humane survival at that) can no longer be geographically confined. While art may be able to provide a temporary escape route from reality, it will not be able to create a lasting alternative: art and the world belong inseparably together.

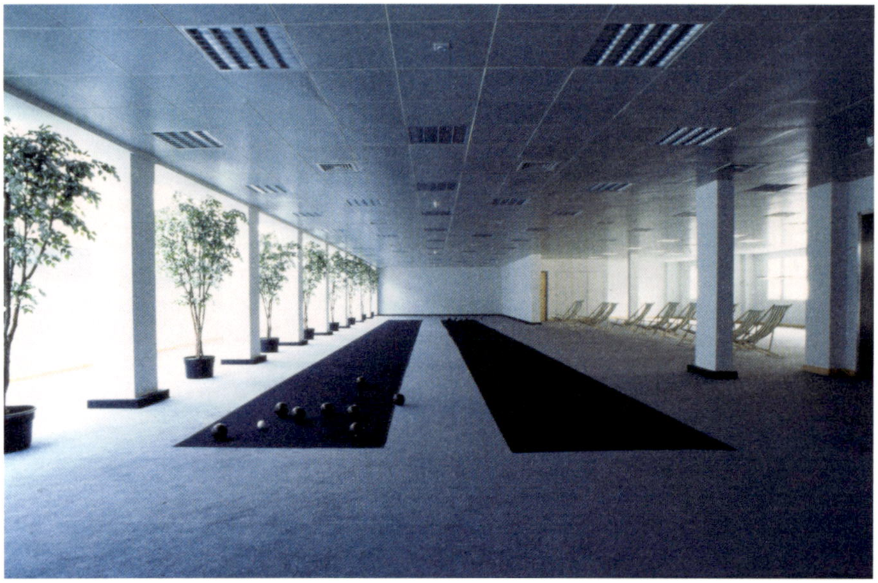

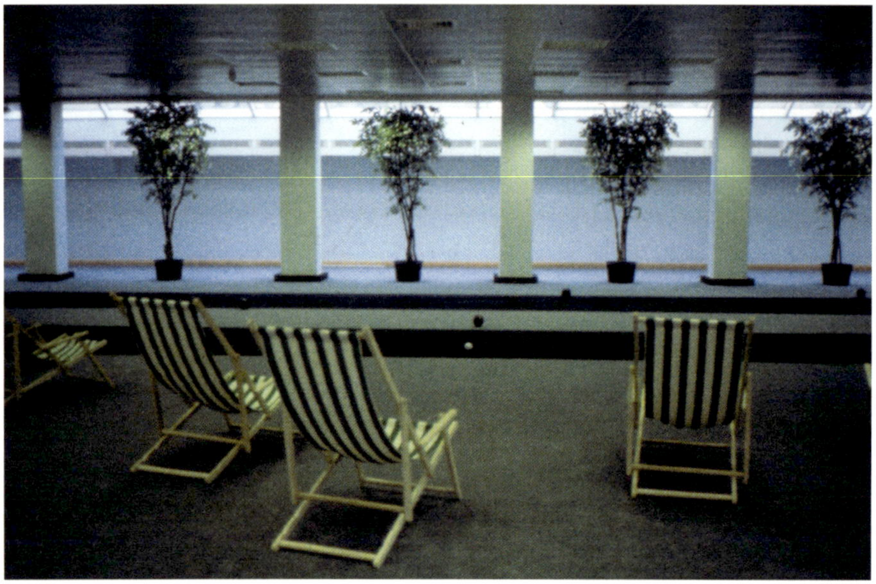

Gabriel Orozco
Empty Club (1996)
Commissioned by Artangel, London
Installation view
The Devonshire Club,
50 St James's Street, London

Notes

1. Benjamin Buchloh, Megan Sullivan, Gabriel Orozco, 'To Make an Inner Time: A Conversation with Gabriel Orozco', *October*, no. 130, autumn 2009, 18.
2. Nikos Papastergiadis, '"Everything That Surrounds": Art Politics and Theories of the Everyday', 1998; reprinted in Stephen Johnstone, ed., *The Everyday* (London: Whitechapel Gallery/MIT Press, 2008) 74.
3. Siegfried Kracauer, *Mass Ornament: Weimar Essays* (Cambridge: Harvard University Press, 1995) 58.
4. Interview with Arturo Herrera, in Roxana Marcoci, *Comic Abstraction: Image-Breaking, Image-Making* (New York: The Museum of Modern Art, 2007) 64.
5. Ben Highmore, *Everyday Life and Cultural Theory*, 2002, reprinted in Johnstone, ed., op.cit., 84.
6. 'Metal Is a Major Thing to Waste: Interview with Cady Noland', *Archis*, January 1994, 79.
7. On the connection between Chan and Duchamp, see also George Baker, 'Paul Chan: The Image from Outside', *Paul Chan. The 7 ~~Lights~~* (London and Cologne: Serpentine Gallery and Verlag der Buchhandlung Walther König, 2007) 4–16.
8. 'Esoteric, useless, dumb, opportunistic… Paul Chan in conversation with Eungie Joo', D. Fogle, ed., *Life on Mars. 55th Carnegie International* (Pittsburgh: Carnegie Museum of Art, 2009) 396.
9. Duchamp dropped one metre-long pieces of string on the ground fixing the resulting curves as one side of wooden rulers which consequently, of course, no longer measured one metre.
10. Kate Bush, 'Only Connect', *Frieze*, no. 83, May 2004, 73.
11. Benjamin Buchloh, Megan Sullivan, Gabriel Orozco, op. cit., 195.
12. Gabriel Orozco in an interview with Benjamin Buchloh, in Francesco Bonami, ed., *Gabriel Orozco: Clinton is Innocent* (Paris: Musée d'Art Moderne de la Ville de Paris, 1998) 174.
13. Cited in Kristin M. Jones, 'Rivane Neuenschwander', *Frieze*, no. 104, January–February 2007, 167.
14. In 1928 Oswald de Andrade (1890–1954), one of the leaders of the Brazilian modernist movement, published the *Manifesto Antropófago* which celebrated the country's ability to absorb influences from the outside. For a more detailed account of the link between *antropófagia* and Neuenschwander's work, see also Daniel Birnbaum, 'Feast for the Eyes: the art of Rivane Neuenschwander' *Art Forum International*, Vol 41, Issue 9, 2003.

Ester Partegàs
It's an Individual Experience
(We the People Series) (2006)
Inkjet Ultrachrome archival
ink print
113 x 130 cm

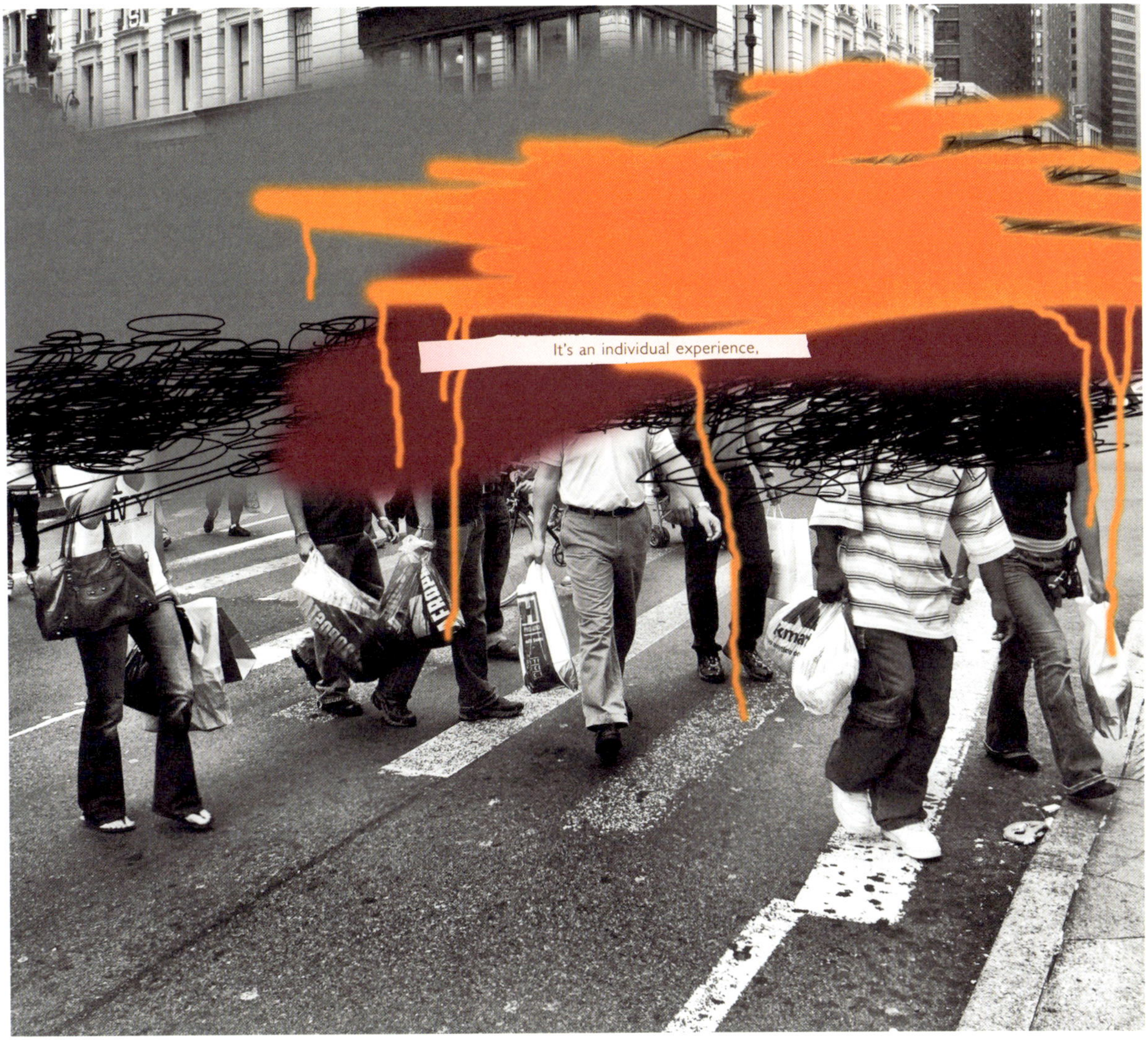
It's an individual experience,

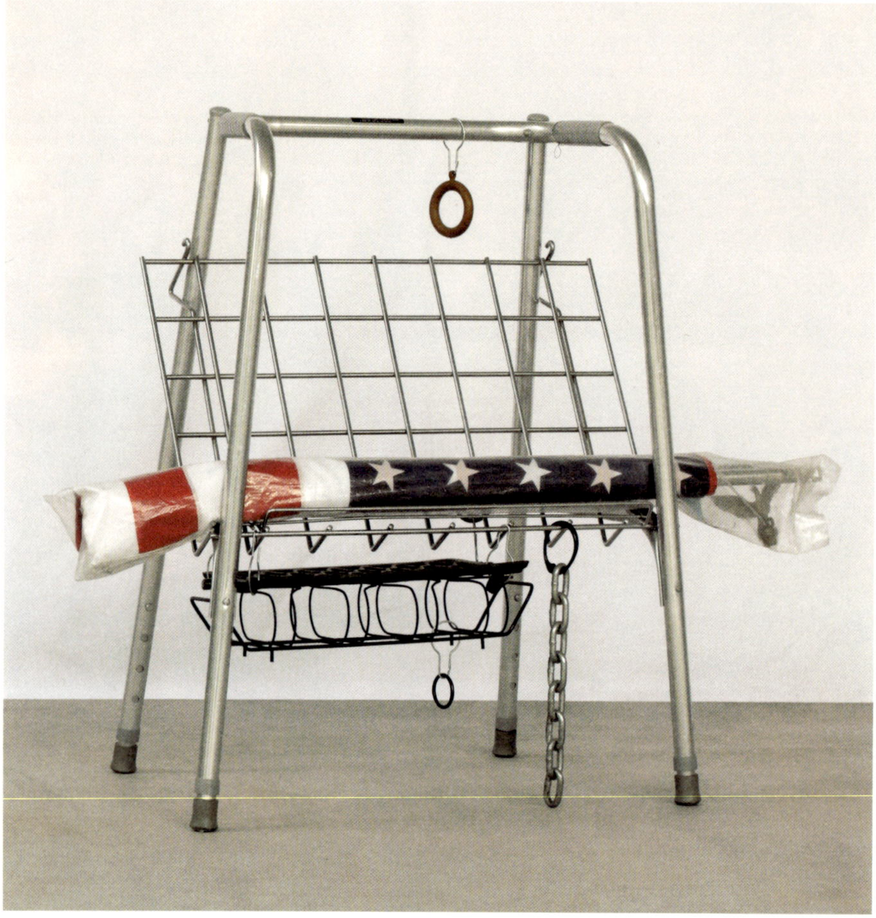

Cady Noland
Objectification Process (1989)
Aluminium walker, wire, metal rings, plastic curtain ring, steel grid, steel rack American flag in plastic, plastic shower curtain rings, vintage iron sewing machine pedal, metal can/bottle rack, steel chain, rubber stopper
79 x 103 x 45 cm

Cowboy Eating, with Holes and Scarf in Crotch Hole (1990)
Silkscreen on aluminium with black polyester cloth
184 x 123 cm

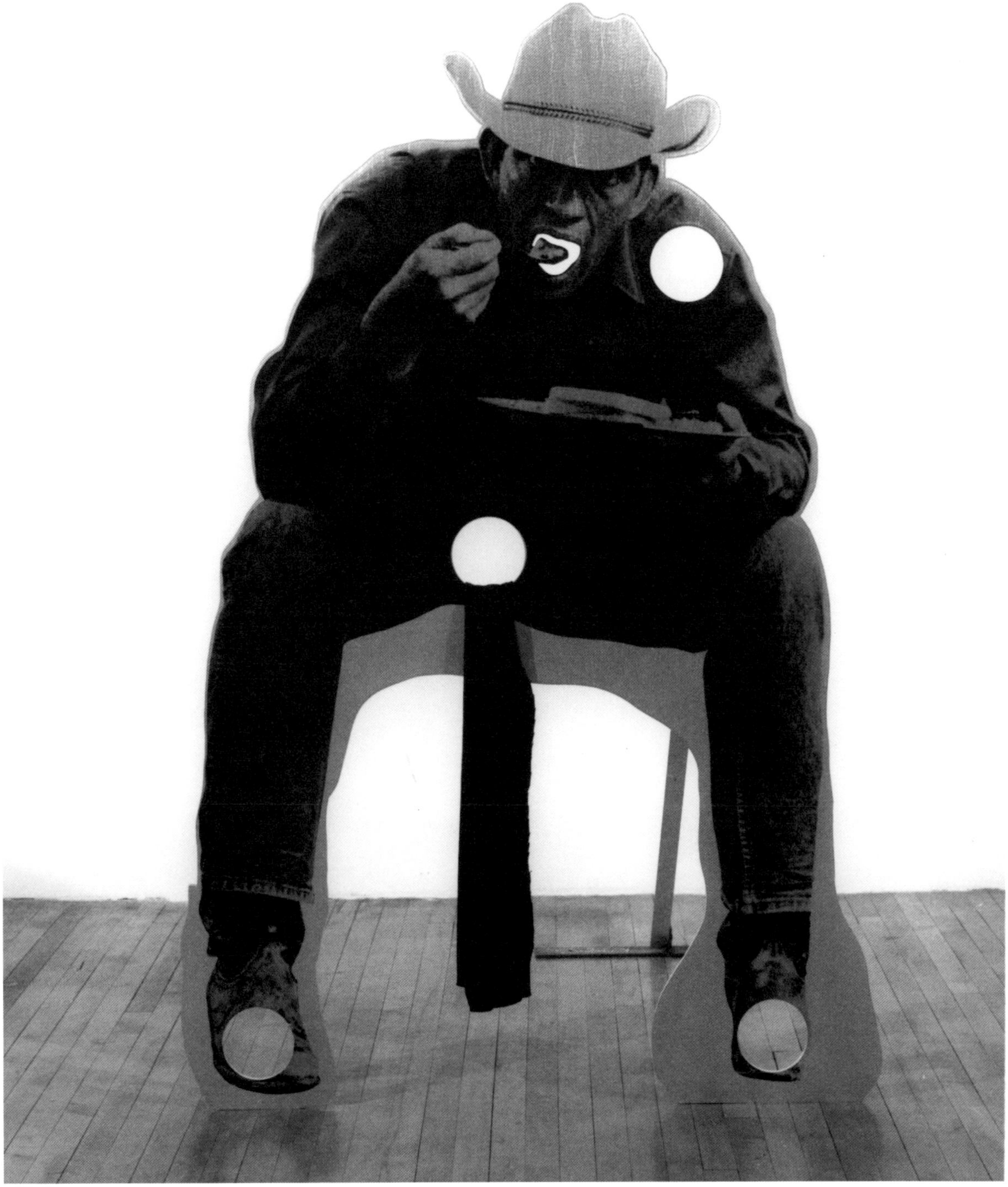

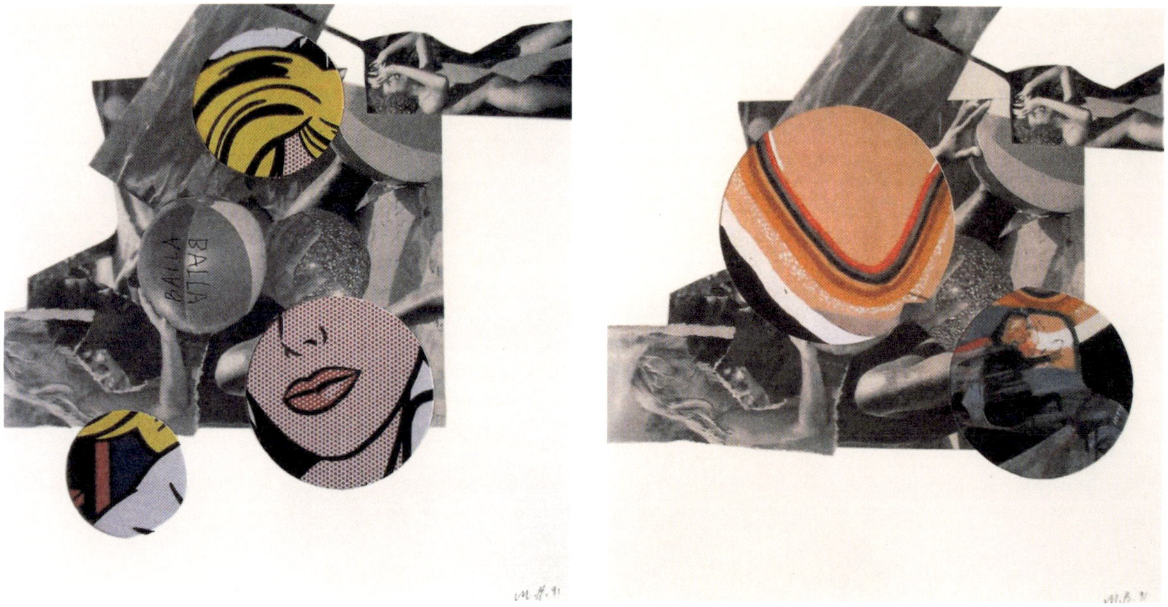

Martin Kippenberger
Pop Art Calendar (1991)
Collage
Each 43.5 x 29 cm

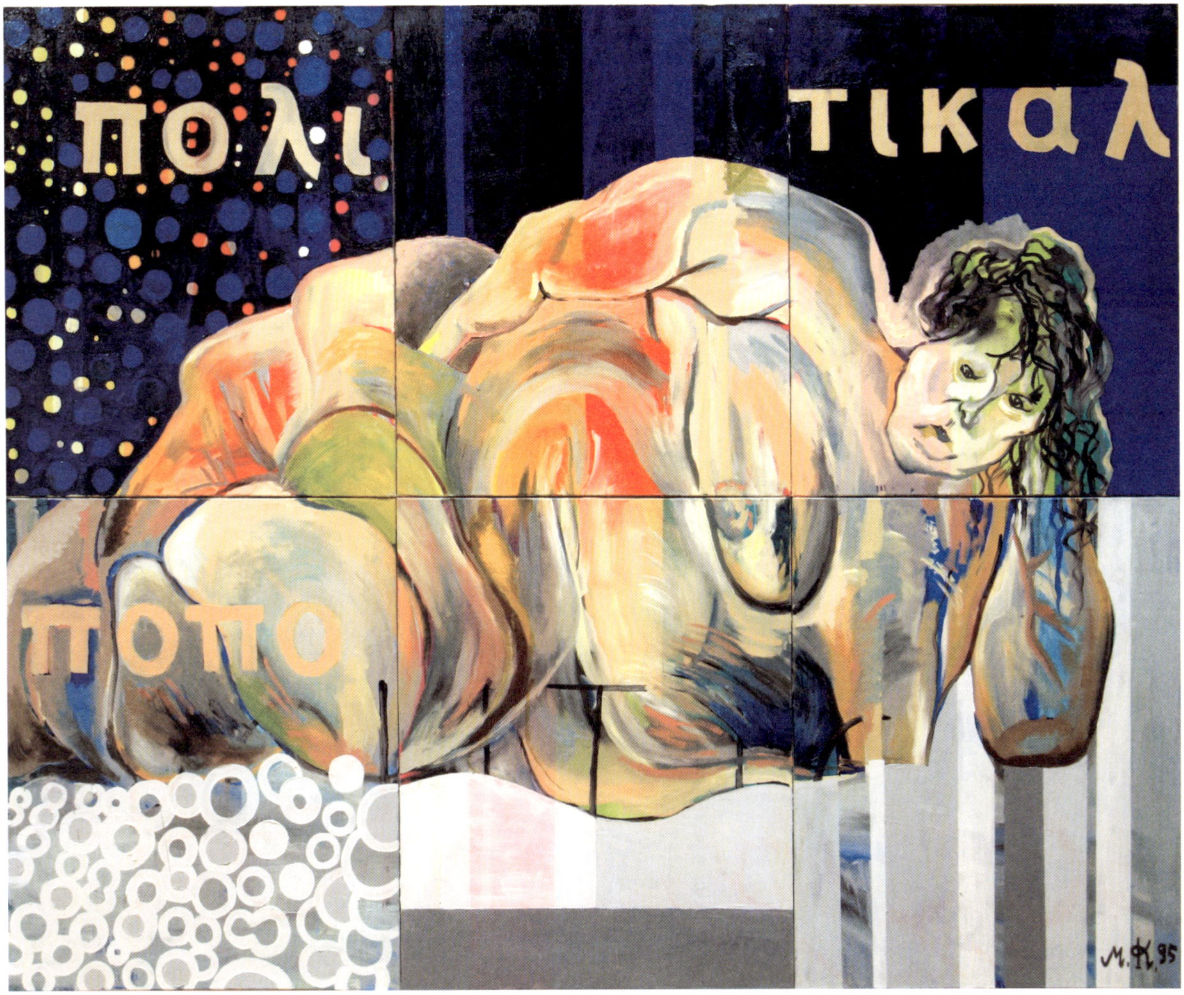

Martin Kippenberger
I Am Too Political (1995)
Oil on canvas
180 x 225 cm

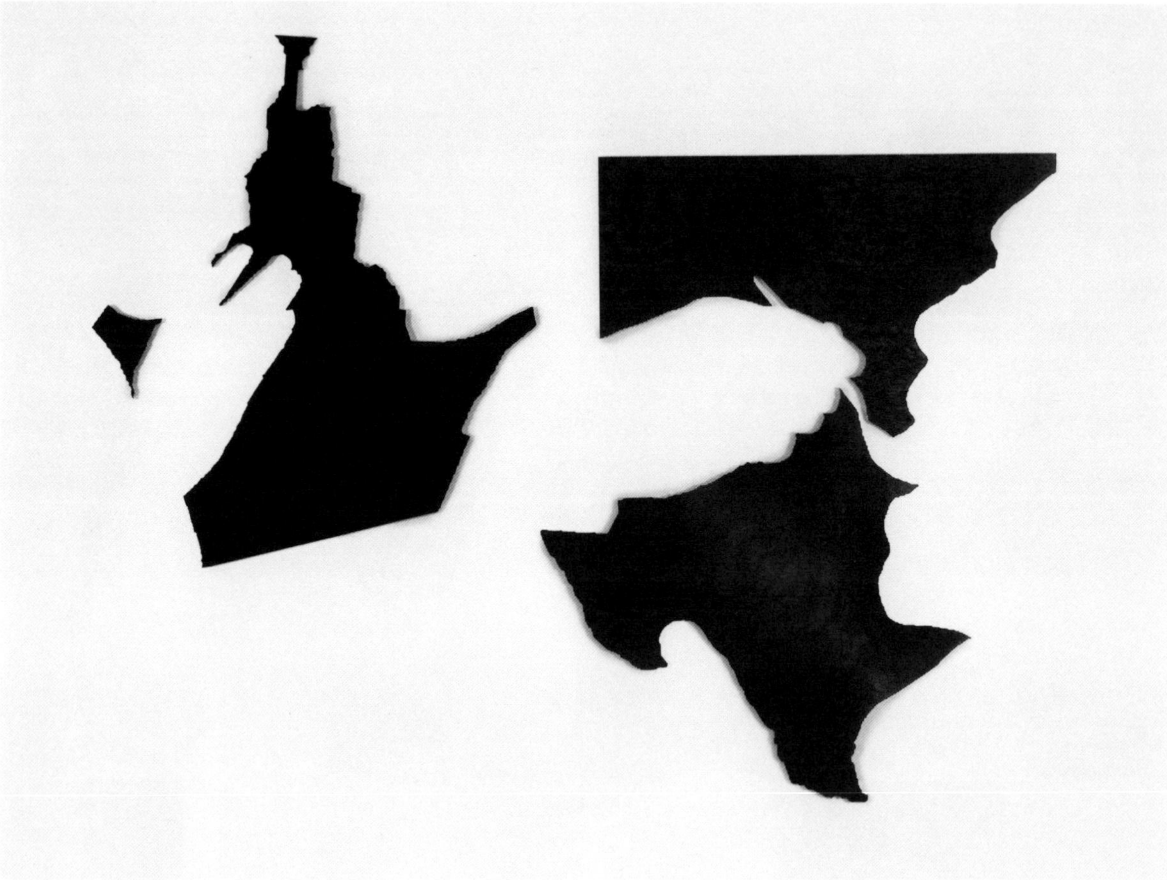

Seth Price
Untitled (whispering – feeding) (2008)
Imbuya and diamond acrylic plastic
330 x 251 cm
4 parts

Sam Durant
La Plus Belle Sculpture (2007)
spray enamel on mirror, plywood
201.6 x 108.9 x 2.5 cm

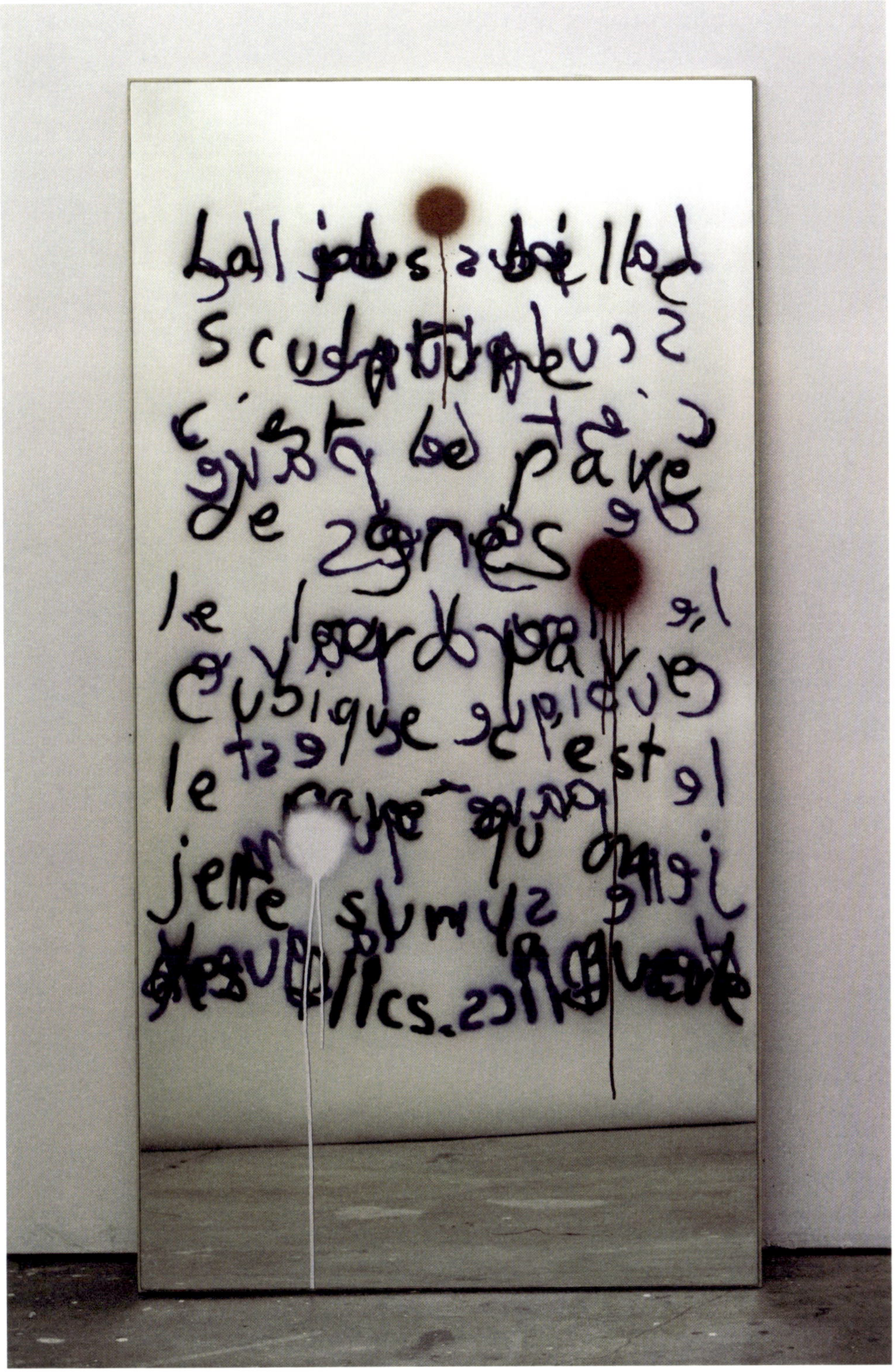

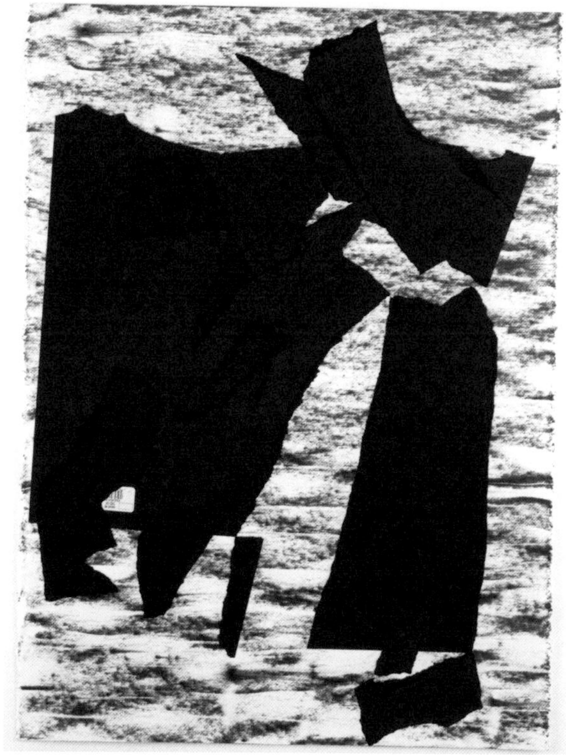

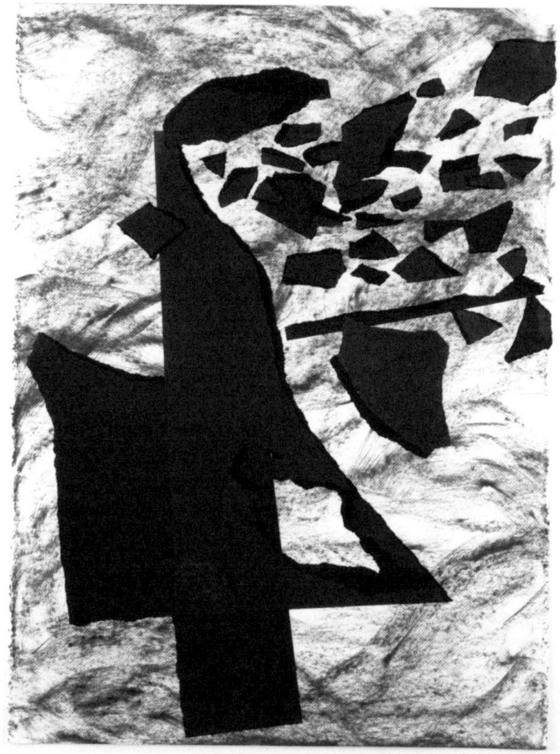

Paul Chan
7th Science and Westerns Today (Measure 63) (2007)
Mixed media on paper
76.2 x 55.9 cm

7th Tropic of Shaker (Measure 56) (2007)
Mixed media on paper
76.2 x 55.9 cm

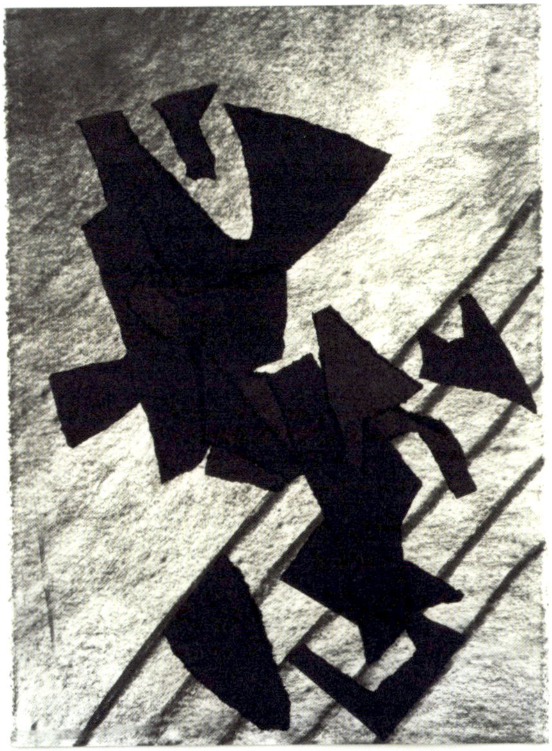

7th Out of Somebody's Body
(Measure 16) (2007)
Mixed media on paper
76.2 x 55.9 cm

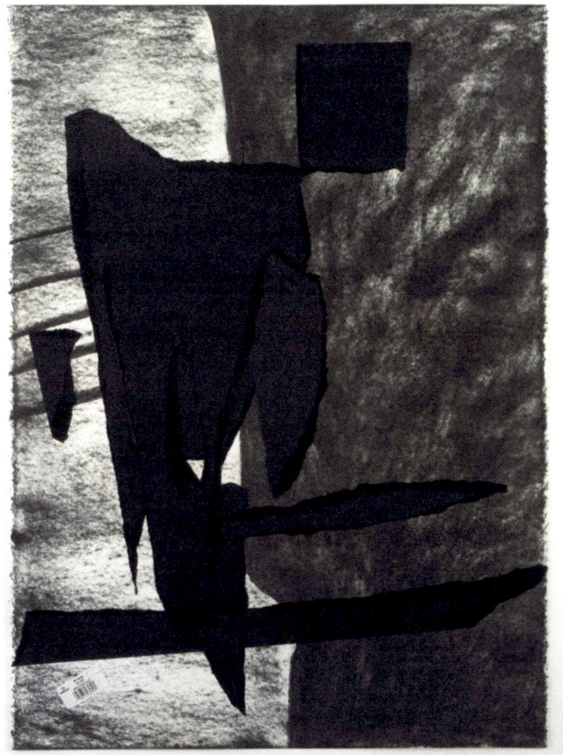

7th Moby Dick/Think
(Measure 169) (2007)
Mixed media on paper
76.2 x 55.9 cm

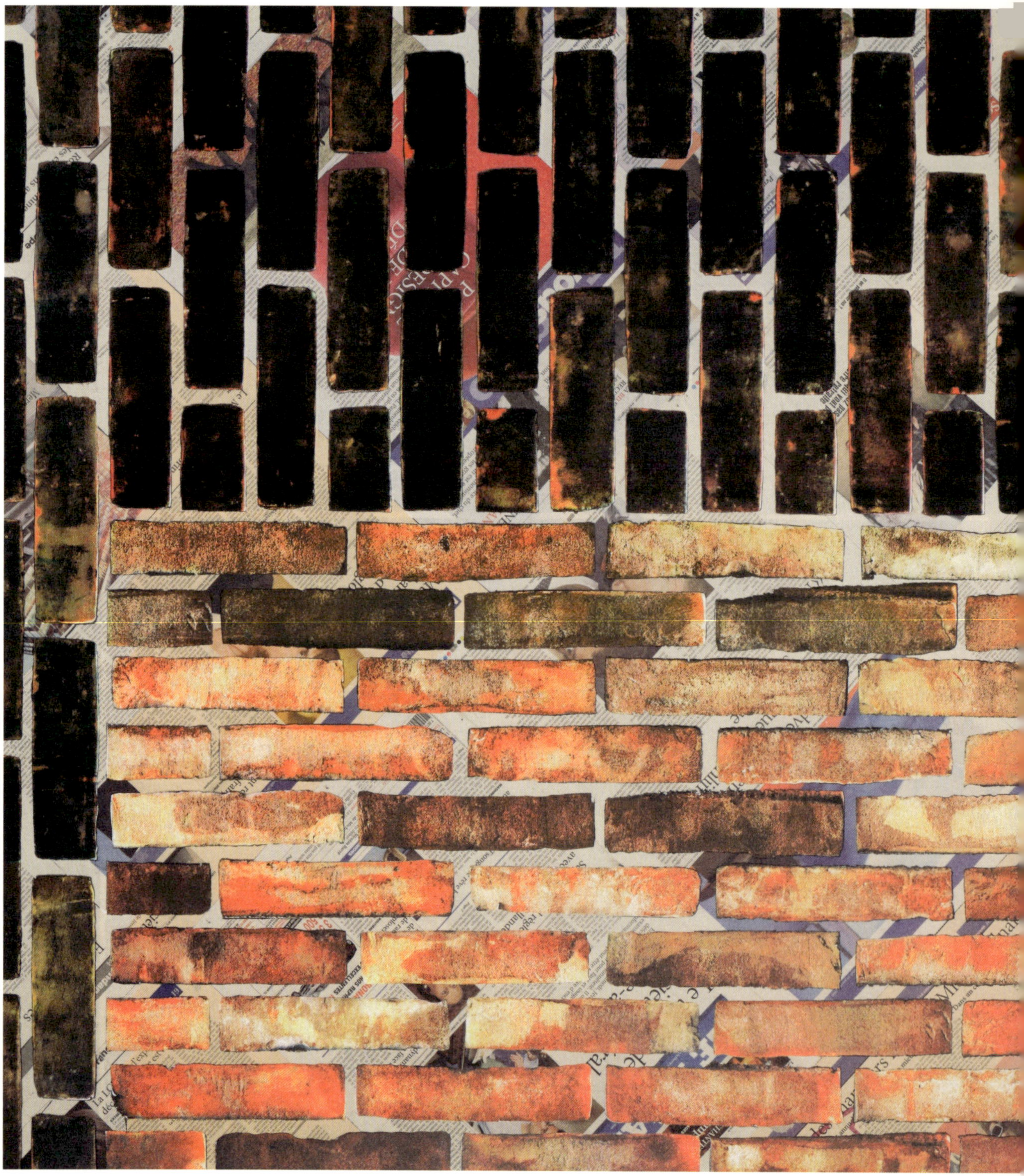

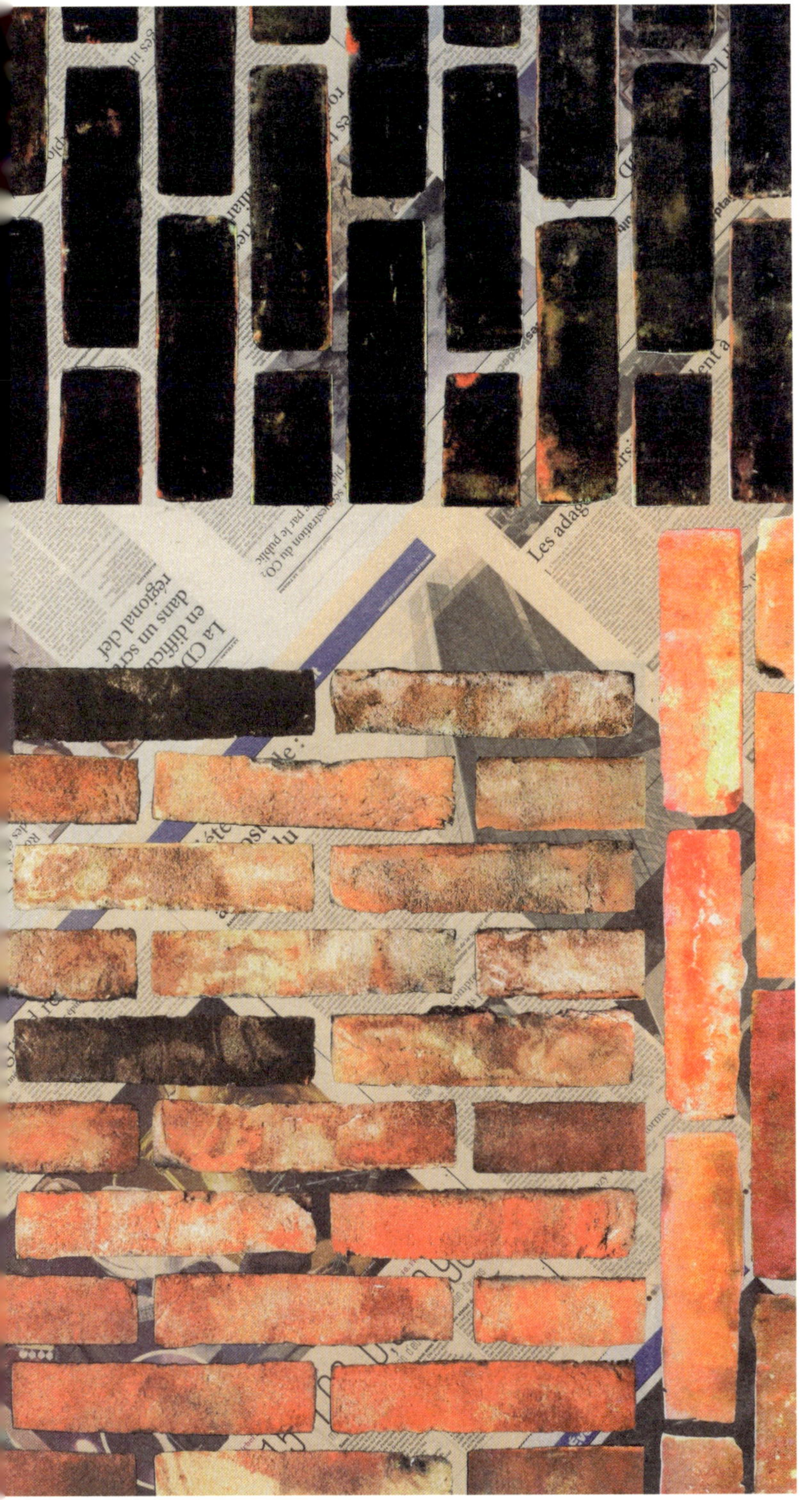

Kelley Walker
Untitled (2008)
Four-colour process silkscreen on canvas with collage of *Le Figaro*, Monday 28 January 2008
121.9 x 243.8 cm

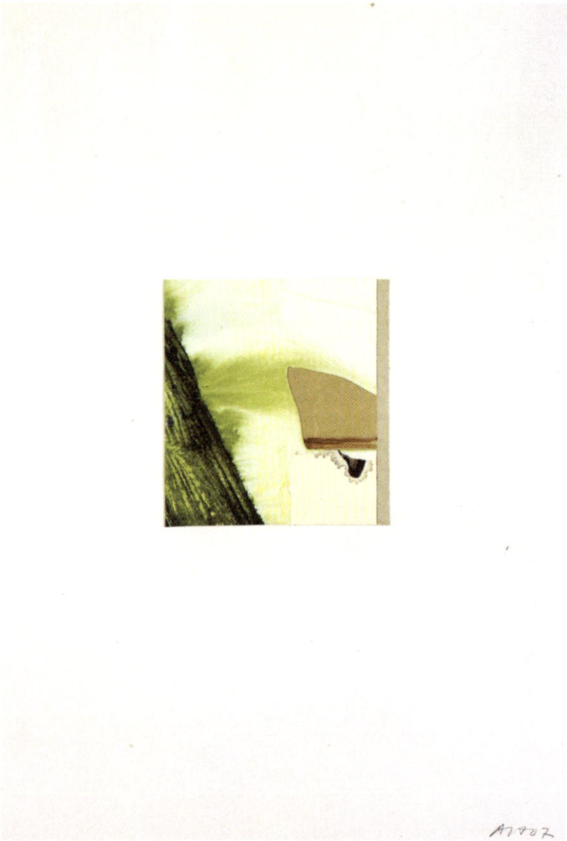

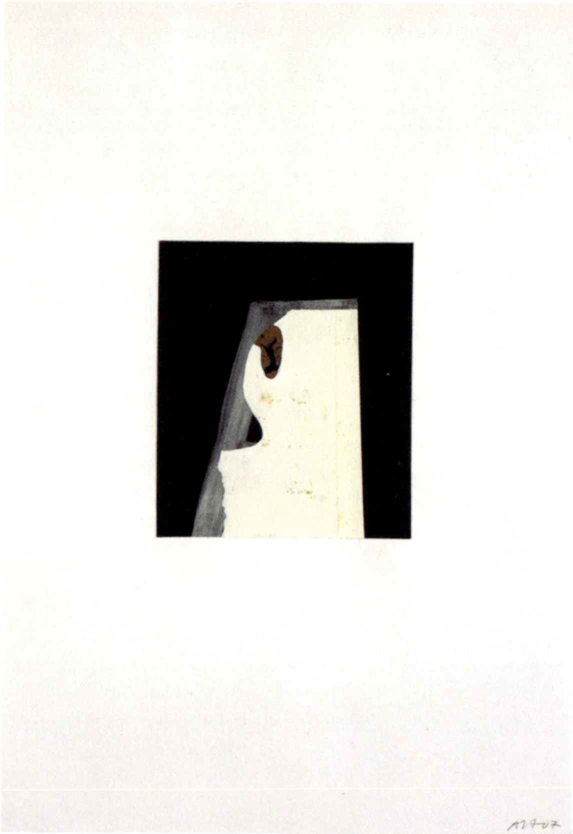

Arturo Herrera
Napule (2007)
Collage, paper, canvas on paper
100 x 70 cm

La Moto (2007)
Collage, paper, canvas on paper
100 x 70 cm

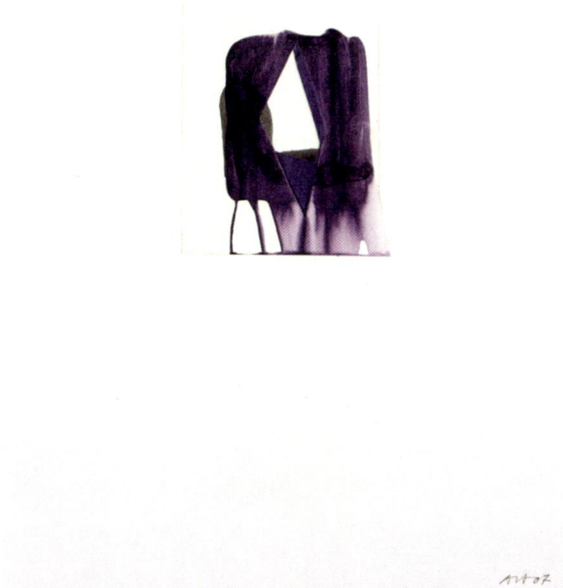

Potsdam (2007)
Collage, paper, canvas on paper
100 x 70 cm

Pedropar (2007)
Collage, paper, canvas on paper
100 x 70 cm

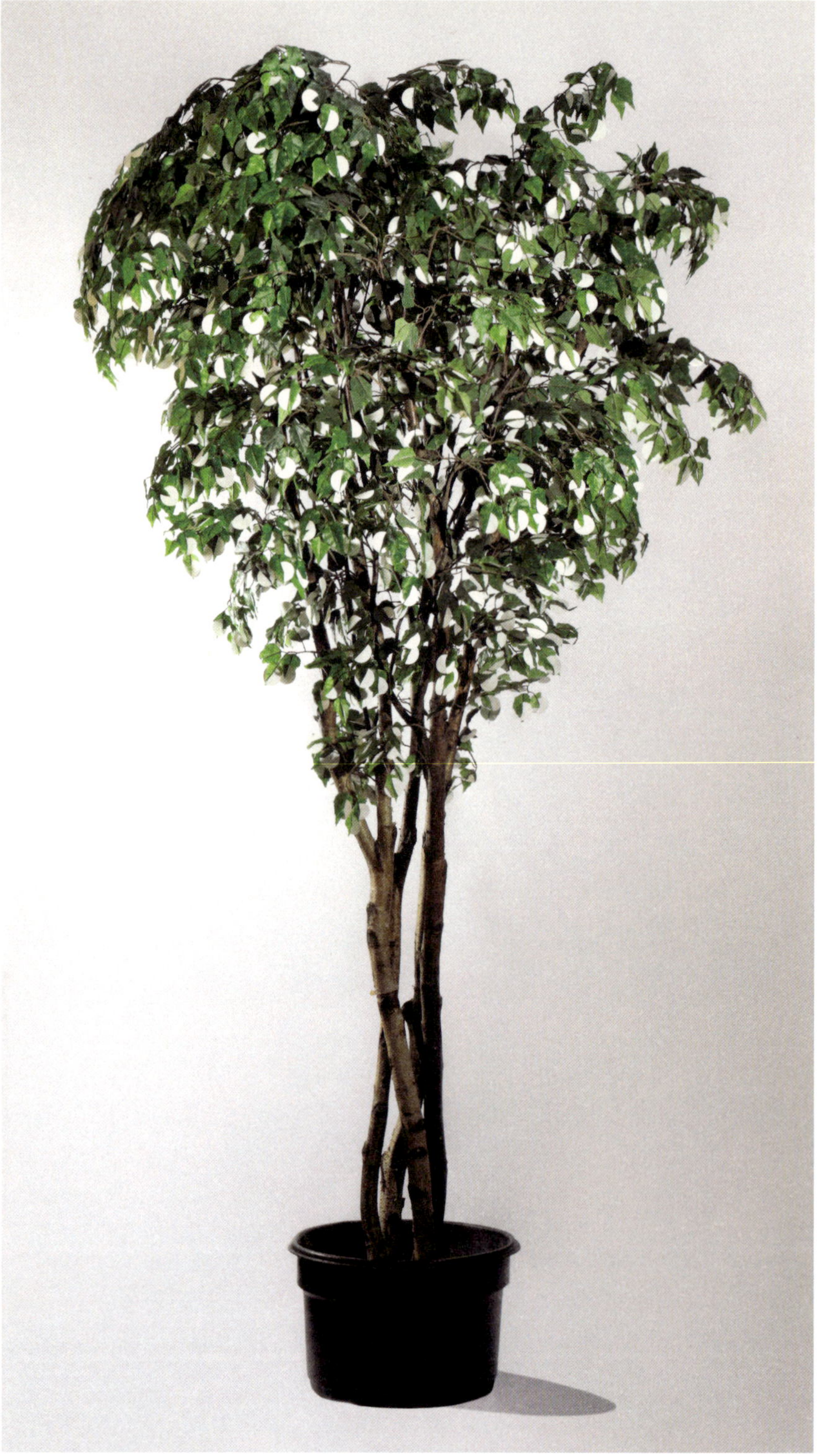

Gabriel Orozco
Moon Tree (1996)
Wood, paper, plastic
Approx.
254 x 167.6 x 167.6 cm

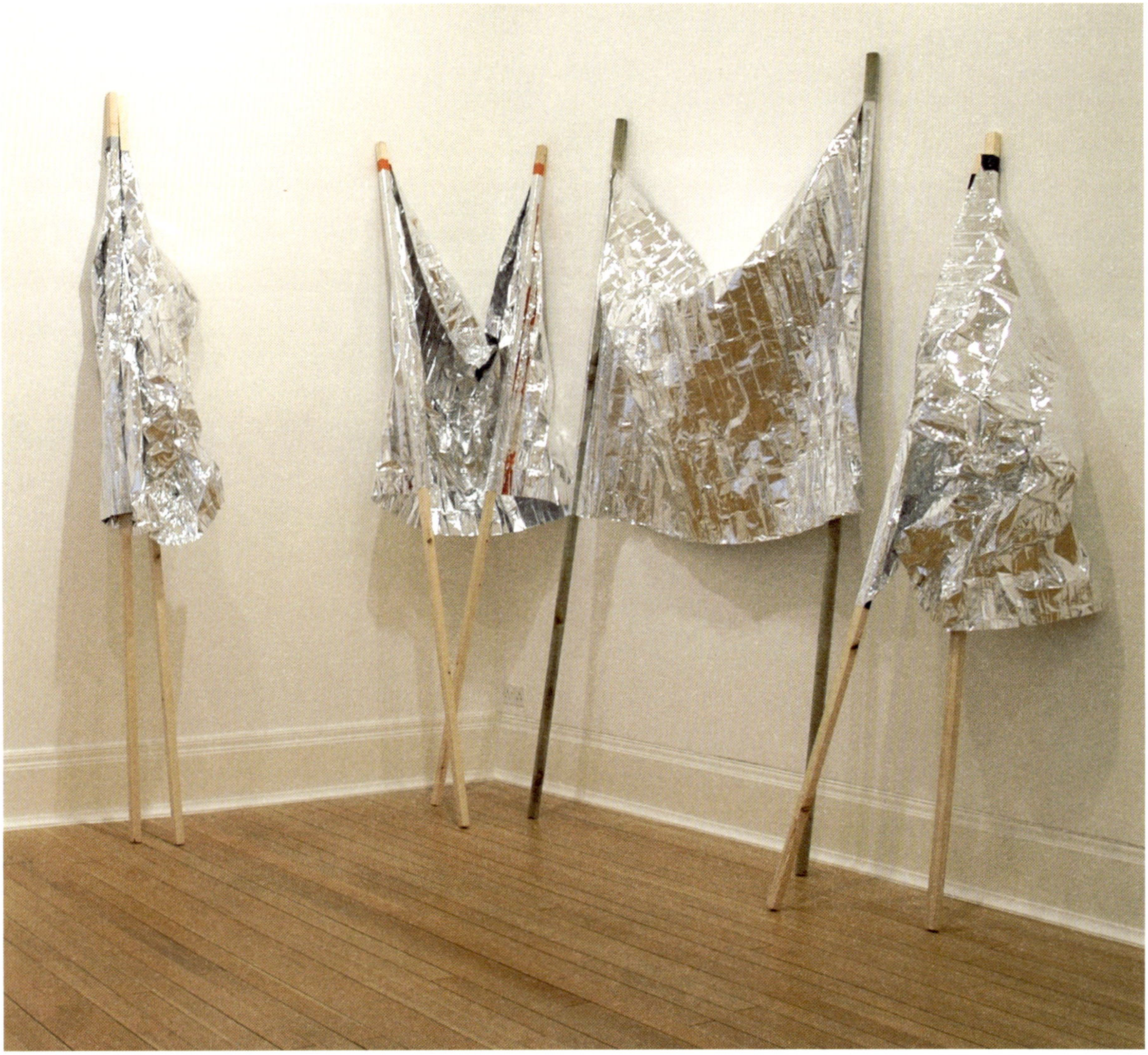

Gabriel Kuri
Quick Standards (2005)
Four emergency blankets taped on wooden sticks (silver, black, weatherproof, orange)
270 cm x dimensions variable

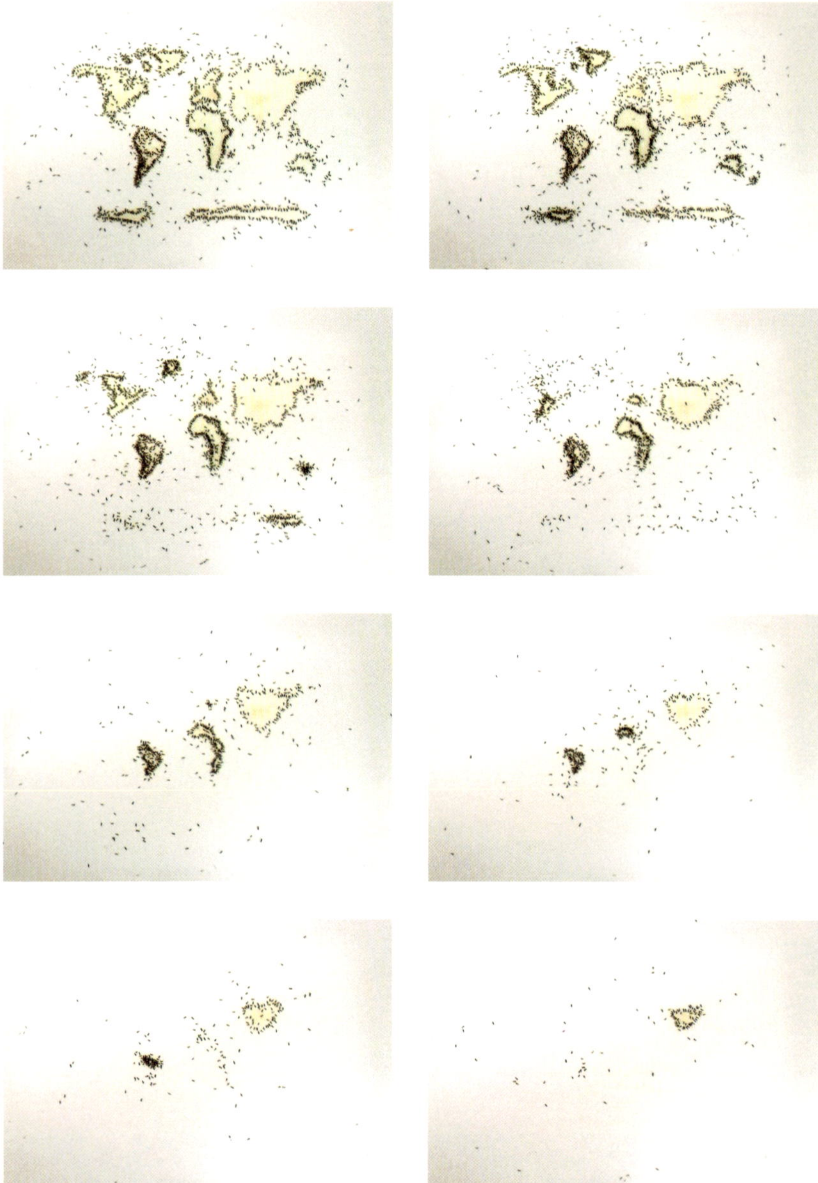

Rivane Neuenschwander
Contingent (2008)
Digital video
Running time: 10'30"

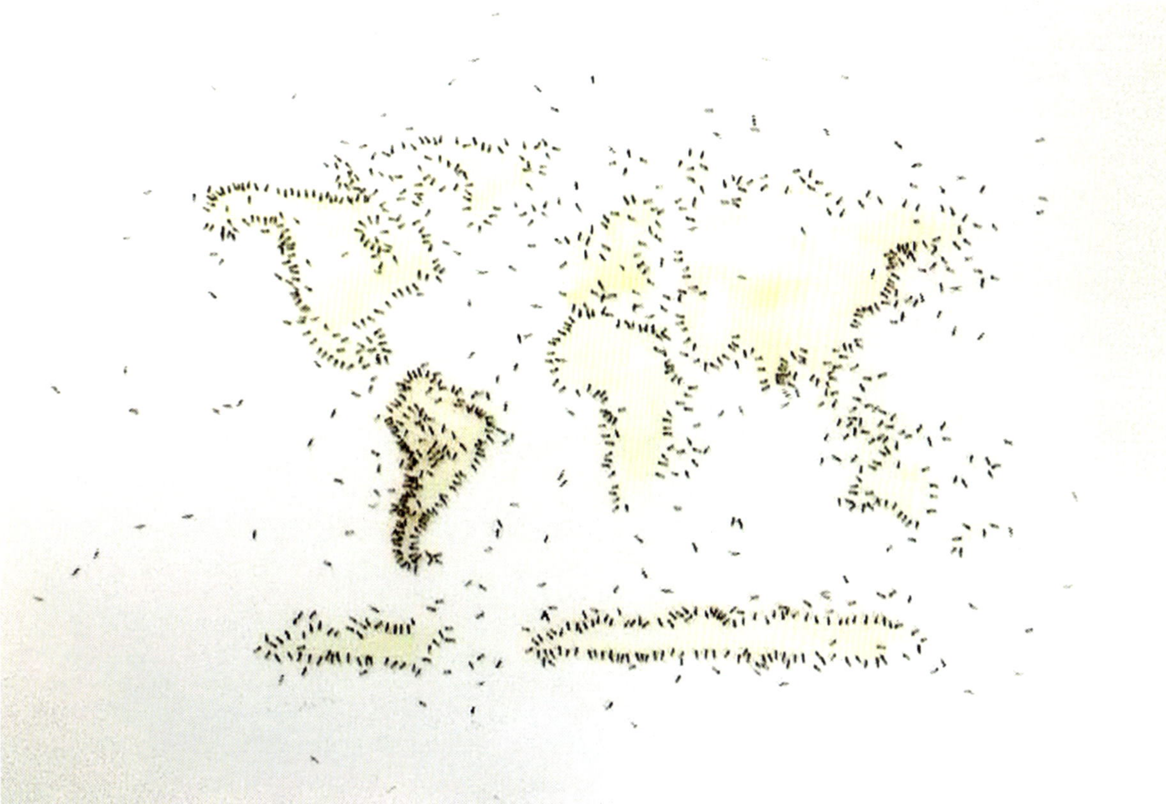

List of works
Further reading
Image credits
Index
Acknowledgements

List of works

Act 1: The Corporeal

Marina Abramović
Born 1946, Belgrade, Yugoslavia. Lives and works in New York, US

Cleaning the Mirror #1 (1995)
Video installation with five television monitors
Dimensions variable

John Bock
Born 1965, Gribbohm, Germany. Lives and works in Berlin, Germany

Winona Ryder (2009)
Curtain with several objects
250 x 200 cm

Louise Bourgeois
Born 1911, Paris, France. Lives and works in New York, US

Fillette (Sweeter Version) (1968–1999)
Latex over plaster
59.6 x 26.6 x 19.6 cm

Marcel Duchamp
Born 1887, Blainville-Crevon, France, died 1968, Neuilly-sur-Seine, France. Lived and worked in Paris, France and New York, US

Fountain (1917/1964)
Glaze cast ceramic urinal with black paint
35.6 x 49.1 x 62.6 cm

Jimmie Durham
Born 1940, Arkansas, US. Lives and works in Berlin, Germany

No one will be harmed. This is only a test (2008)
Metal, wood
180 x 51 x 65 cm

Robert Gober
Born 1954, Connecticut, US. Lives and works in New York, US

A Pair of Basinless Sinks (1986)
Plaster, wood, wire lath, semi-gloss enamel paint
68.6 x 168.9 x 6.6 cm

Untitled (1991)
Beeswax with hair, pigment
61 x 40 x 31 cm

Untitled (2000)
Lithograph, screen print, mixed media on paper
55.9 x 81.3 cm

David Hammons
Born 1943, Illinois, US. Lives and works in New York, US

Untitled (1974)
Body print
34.3 x 29.2 cm

Untitled (1975)
Body print
106.7 x 78.7 cm

Untitled (Hair Piece) (1975–1976)
Wire, hair
97.8 x 31.8 cm

Blue Angels (Penises), (c.1970s)
Body print
29.7 x 37.7 cm

Jim Hodges
Born 1957, Spokane, US. Lives and works in New York, US

Untitled (Everything So Alive Lively Living) (2006)
Ink saliva transfer on paper
152.4 x 111.8 cm

Despina Isaia
Born 1974, Athens, Greece. Lives and works in Athens, Greece

Untitled (2003)
Crochet with the artist's hair, sequins
75 x 100 cm

Sherrie Levine
Born 1947, Pennsylvania, US. Lives and works in New York, US

Fountain (Buddha): 5 (1996)
Cast bronze
42.5 x 40 x 30 cm

Body Mask (2007)
Cast bronze
57.2 x 24.1 x 14.6 cm

Sarah Lucas
Born 1962, London, UK. Lives and works in Suffolk, UK

Bunny Gets Snookered #10 (1997)
Tan tights, red stockings, chair, steel clamp, kapok, wire
104 x 71 x 89 cm

Kiki Smith
Born 1954, Nuremberg, Germany. Lives and works in New York, US

Untitled (1980–92)
Four lightboxes
Dimensions variable

Paul Thek
Born 1933, New York, US, died 1988, New York, US. Lived and worked in New York, US

Untitled (Meat Cable) (1969)
Wax, paint, steel cables with turnbuckles
Length: 345.5 cm

Sue Williams
Born 1954, Chicago, US. Lives and works New York, US

Family Room (1994)
Ink on white paper from spiral block, collage on printed paper
30 x 44 cm

Busy With Calm Background (1995)
Ink on white paper, collage on wallpaper
44.5 x 33 cm

Creamy Floral (1995)
Ink on wallpaper
44.5 x 33 cm

Act 2: Subversive Abstraction

Lynda Benglis
Born 1941, Louisiana, US. Lives and works in New York and Santa Fe, US; Kastelorizo, Greece and Ahmedabad, India

Très (1976)
Wire mesh, cotton bunting, plaster, sprayed aluminium, copper
61 x 152.4 x 30.5 cm

Robert Gober
Born 1954, Connecticut, US. Lives and works in New York, US

Unfolding Door (1989)
Enamel on wood, steel
85 x 85 x 47 cm

David Hammons
Born 1943, Illinois, US. Lives and works in New York, US

Untitled (from Flight Fantasy) (1995)
Paint, custom rollers, heavy metal wire hoops, human hair, crystals, netting
Dimensions variable

Damien Hirst
Born 1965, Bristol, UK. Lives and works in London and Devon, UK

Untitled (Collage 2) (1985)
Mixed media
69 x 46 cm

Mike Kelley
Born 1954, Detroit, US. Lives in Los Angeles, US

Transplant (1990)
Mixed media
343 x 77 cm

Nikos Kessanlis
Born 1930, Thessaloniki, Greece, died 2004, Athens, Greece. Lived and worked Rome, Italy; Paris, France and Athens, Greece

Untitled (Gesture) (1961)
Readymade object, tissue, wire
200 x 21 cm

Julie Mehretu
Born 1970, Addis Ababa, Ethiopia. Lives and works in New York, US

Untitled (2006)
Graphite, ink, watercolour on paper
71.1 x 101.6 cm

Untitled (2006)
Graphite, ink, watercolour on paper
66 x 101.6 cm

Kori Newkirk
Born 1970, New York, US. Lives in Los Angeles, US

Virgil (2002)
Braids, aluminium, beads, dye
166 x 122 cm

Dieter Roth
Born 1930, Hannover, Germany, died 1998, Basel, Switzerland. Lived and worked in Reykjavik, Iceland; Stuttgart, Düsseldorf, Cologne and Berlin, Germany; London, UK; Vienna, Austria; Zurich, Switzerland and Los Angeles, US

Grafik mit Kakao (1969)
Screenprint with chocolate in a plastic wrapper
70 x 100 cm

Grosse Landschaft (1969)
Pressed cheese on roofing felt within artist's frame
98 x 65.3 cm

Kleine Landschaft (1969)
Cheese on sandpaper in plastic sleeve
32 x 43.5 cm

Daniel Subkoff
Born 1974, New York, US. Lives and works in New York, US

All Her Clothes Are Swept Aside by Her Face (2008)
Canvas
200 x 300 cm/
dimensions variable

Rosemarie Trockel
Born 1952, Schwerte, Germany. Lives and works in Cologne, Germany

Avalanche (2008)
Glazed ceramic, metal
113 x 53 x 38 cm

Something of Tomorrow 1 (2008)
Mixed media
68 x 58 x 5 cm

Act 3: Current Disturbance

Mona Hatoum
Born 1952, Beirut, Lebanon. Lives and works in London, UK and Berlin, Germany

Current Disturbance (1996)
Wood, wire mesh, light bulbs, computerized dimmer switch, amplifier, four speakers
279 x 550.5 x 504 cm

Act 4: Material Intelligence

Paul Chan
Born 1973, Hong Kong, China. Lives and works in New York, US

7th Out of Somebody's Body (Measure 16) (2007)
Mixed media on paper
76.2 x 55.9 cm

7th Tropic of Shaker (Measure 56) (2007)
Mixed media on paper
76.2 x 55.9 cm

7th Science and Westerns Today (Measure 63) (2007)
Mixed media on paper
76.2 x 55.9 cm

7th Moby Dick/Think (Measure 169) (2007)
Mixed media on paper
76.2 x 55.9 cm

Sam Durant
Born 1961, Seattle, US. Live and works in California, US

La Plus Belle Sculpture (2007)
Spray enamel on mirror, plywood
201.6 x 108.9 x 2.5 cm

Arturo Herrera
Born 1959, Caracas, Venezuela. Lives and works in Berlin, Germany

La Moto (2007)
Collage, paper, canvas on paper
100 x 70 cm

Napule (2007)
Collage, paper, canvas on paper
100 x 70 cm

Pedropar (2007)
Collage, paper, canvas on paper
100 x 70 cm

Potsdam (2007)
Collage, paper, canvas on paper
100 x 70 cm

Martin Kippenberger
Born 1953, Dortmund, Germany, died 1997, Vienna, Austria. Lived and worked in Vienna, Austria

I Am Too Political (1995)
Oil on canvas
180 x 225 cm

Pop Art Calendar (1991)
12 collages
Each 43.5 x 29 cm

Gabriel Kuri
Born 1970, Mexico City, Mexico. Lives and works in Mexico City, Mexico and Brussels, Belgium

Quick Standards (2005)
Four emergency blankets taped on wooden sticks (silver, black, weatherproof, orange)
270 cm x dimensions variable

Rivane Neuenschwander
Born 1967, Belo Horizonte, Brazil. Lives and works in Belo Horizonte, Brazil

Contingent (2008)
Digital video
Running time: 10'30"

Cady Noland
Born 1956, Washington, D.C, US. Lives and works in New York, US

Cowboy Eating, with Holes and Scarf in Crotch Hole (1990)
Silkscreen on aluminium with black polyester cloth
184 x 123 cm

Objectification Process (1989)
Aluminium walker, wire, metal rings, plastic curtain ring, steel grid, steel rack, American flag in plastic, plastic shower curtain rings, vintage iron sewing machine pedal, metal can/bottle rack, steel chain, rubber stopper
79 x 103 x 45 cm

Gabriel Orozco
Born 1962, Veracruz, Mexico. Lives and works in New York, US; Paris, France and Mexico City, Mexico

Moon Tree (1996)
Wood, paper, plastic
Approx.
254 x 167.6 x 167.6 cm

Ester Partegàs
Born 1972, Barcelona, Spain. Lives and works in New York, US

It's an Individual Experience (We the People Series) (2006)
Inkjet Ultrachrome archival ink print
113 x 130 cm

Seth Price
Born 1973, East Jerusalem, Palestine. Lives and works in New York, US

Untitled (whispering – feeding) (2008)
Imbuya and diamond acrylic plastic
330 x 251 cm

Kelley Walker
Born 1969, Georgia, US. Lives and works in New York, US

Untitled (2008)
Four-colour process silkscreen on canvas with collage of *Le Figaro*, Monday 28 January 2008
121.9 x 243.8 cm

Further reading

Bruce J. Altshuler, ed., *Collecting the New: Museums and Contemporary Art* (Princeton: Princeton University Press, 2005)

Walter Benjamin, 'Unpacking My Library: A Talk about Book Collecting' in Walter Benjamin, *Illuminations*, Hannah Arendt, ed., (New York: Schocken Books, 1968)

Benjamin H.D. Buchloh, *Neo-Avantgarde and Culture Industry: Essays on European and American Art from 1955 to 1975* (Cambridge MA and London: MIT Press, 2000)

Martha Buskirk and Mignon Nixon, eds., *The Duchamp Effect* (Cambridge MA and London: MIT Press, 1996)

Thierry de Duve, *Résonances du Readymade: Duchamp Entre Avant-garde et Tradition* (London: Hachette Littératures, 1989)

Hal Foster, *The Return of the Real: The Avant-Garde at the End of the Century* (Cambridge MA and London: MIT Press, 1996)

Stephen Johnstone, ed., *The Everyday* (London: Whitechapel Gallery/MIT Press, 2008)

Stephen Melville, ed., *The Lure of the Object* (Yale: Yale University Press, 2006)

John Roberts, *The Intangibilities of Form: Skill and Deskilling in Art After the Readymade* (London: Verso, 2007)

Image credits

Cover: © Sherrie Levine
Courtesy Paula Cooper Gallery, New York
Photo: Tom Powel

14: © Succession Marcel Duchamp/ADAGP Paris/OSDEETE Athens 2010
© Georgia O' Keeffe Museum /Artists Rights Society (ARS), New York/OSDEETE Athens 2010

20: © Robert Gober
Collection Walker Art Center, Minneapolis, T. B. Walker Acquisition Fund, 1992

22: © Robert Mapplethorpe Foundation, published Summer 1989

27–28: All images:
© Succession Marcel Duchamp/ADAGP Paris/OSDEETE Athens 2010.
Photo: Sotheby's Images

29: © Sherrie Levine
Courtesy Paula Cooper Gallery, New York
Photo: Tom Powel

30: © Sherrie Levine
Courtesy Paula Cooper Gallery, New York
Photo: Ellen Page Wilson

31: © Robert Gober
Photo: Nikos Markou

32: © Robert Gober
Photo: Gemini G.E.L.

33: © Robert Gober

34: © Louise Bourgeois
Photo: Christie's Images Ltd.

35–38: All images:
© David Hammons
Photo: Alexandros Filippidis

39: © Jim Hodges
Courtesy Stephen Friedman Gallery, London; Gladstone Gallery, New York and Anthony Meier Fine Arts, San Francisco
Photo: Stephen White

40: © Sue Williams

41: © Sue Williams
Photo: Alexandros Filippidis

42–43: Both images:
© Estate of George Paul Thek
Courtesy Alexander and Bonin, New York
Photo: Bill Orcutt

44–45: © Despina Isaia
Courtesy Els Hanappe Underground
Photo: Vivianna Athanassopoulou

46: © Kiki Smith
Courtesy PaceWildenstein, New York

47: © Marina Abramović/ The Solomon R. Guggenheim Foundation, New York
Courtesy Sean Kelly Gallery, New York
Photo: Kathryn Carr

48: © John Bock

49: © Sarah Lucas
Courtesy Sadie Coles HQ, London

50–51: Both images:
© Jimmie Durham
Courtesy kurimanzutto, Mexico City
Photo: Michel Zabé

57–58: All images:
© John Ranard/Ranard Family Estate
Photo: Nikos Markou

62–63: © David Hammons
Photo: Nikki Johnson

64–65: © David Hammons
Photo: Angus Mill

66: © Lynda Benglis
Courtesy Cheim & Read, New York

67: © Robert Gober

68: © Daniel Subkoff
Photo: Daniel Subkoff

69: © Kori Newkirk
Photo: Nikos Markou

70: Both images:
© Dieter Roth Estate
Photo: Alexandros Filippidis

71: © Dieter Roth Estate

72: © Damien Hirst.
All rights reserved, DACS 2010

73: © Nikos Kessanlis
Courtesy Alpha Delta Gallery, Athens
Photo: Nikos Markou

74–75: © Mike Kelley
Photo: Nikos Markou

76–77: Both images:
© Rosemarie Trockel, VG Bild-Kunst, Bonn 2010

78–79: Both images:
© Julie Mehretu
Courtesy carlier I gebauer

83: Top: © Mona Hatoum
Photo: Patrick Gilbert
Bottom: © Mona Hatoum
Photo: Edward Woodman

84: © Bruce Nauman/Artists Rights Society (ARS), New York/OSDEETE Athens 2010
Courtesy Sperone Westwater, New York

86–91: All images:
© Mona Hatoum
Courtesy White Cube, London and Alexander and Bonin, New York
Photos: Ben Blackwell

97: © Kelley Walker
Courtesy Paula Cooper Gallery, New York
Photo: Nikos Markou

100: Both images:
© Gabriel Orozco
Courtesy Artangel, London
Photo: Stephen White

103: © Ester Partegàs
Courtesy Galería Helga de Alvear, Madrid

104: © Cady Noland
Photo: Nikos Markos

105: © Cady Noland

106–107: Both images:
© Estate Martin Kippenberger
Courtesy Galerie Gisela Capitain, Cologne

108: © Seth Price
Courtesy Galerie Gisela Capitain, Cologne

109: © Sam Durant
Courtesy Paula Cooper Gallery, New York, Sadie Coles HQ, London, Blum & Poe, Los Angeles, and Praz-Delavallade, Paris
Photo: Joshua White

110–111: All images:
© Paul Chan
Courtesy Greene Naftali Gallery, New York
Photo: Jason Mandella

112–113: © Kelley Walker
Courtesy Paula Cooper Gallery, New York
Photo: Nikos Markou

114–115: All images:
© Arturo Herrera
Courtesy Thomas Dane Gallery, London and Sikkema Jenkins, New York

116: © Gabriel Orozco
Courtesy Marian Goodman Gallery, New York
Photo: Nikos Markou

117: © Gabriel Kuri
Courtesy kurimanzutto, Mexico
Photo: Thierry Bal

118–119: Both images:
© Rivane Neuenschwander
Courtesy Stephen Friedman Gallery, London; Tanya Bonakdar Gallery, New York and Galeria Fortes Vilaça, São Paulo

Index

Figures in italics indicate images

Abramović, Marina 23
Cleaning the Mirror #1 23, *47*
Abstract Expressionism 54, 55
abstraction 14, 23, 54, 55, 56, 60, 98
Alberti, Leon Battista 55
American Society of Independent Artists 12
anti-art 59, 60
antropofógia 99
Arp, Jean 20
assemblage 59, 60

Baldessari, John 95
Bauhaus 59
Bellmer, Hans 23
Benglis, Lynda 54, 55
Très 55, *66*
Bentham, Jeremy 84
Beuys, Joseph
The Honey Pump 23
Bill, Max 56
Blake, Peter 95
Bock, John 23
Meechbuildings 23
Winona Ryder 23, *48*
body prints 24, *35*, *36*, *37*
Bourgeois, Louise 13, 21
Fillette (Sweet Version) 21, *34*
Brancusi, Constantin 20–21
Braque, Georges 54
Buren, Daniel 56

Cannon, Steve 56
Chan, Paul 96, 98
7th Moby Dick/Think (Measure 169) 111
7th Out of Somebody's Body (Measure 16) 111
7th Science and Westerns Today (Measure 63) 110
7th Tropic of Shaker (Measure 56) 110
Lights series 96
collage 12, 21, 23, *40*, *41*, 59, *72*, 95, 96, 98, *106*, *113*, *114*, *115*
Conceptual art 18
concrete art 56
Constructivism 12, 55
Russian 60
Cubism 12, 18, 54
Cueff, Alain 13

D. Daskalopoulos Collection 13, 14
Dada 12, 54, 59, 60
date paintings 96
De Kooning, Willem 21
Deutsche Bank 96
Documenta (1977) 23
drawings 23, 59, 60
Duchamp, Marcel 12–13, 19, 20–21, 60, 95, 98, 99
3 Standard Stoppages 98
Drain Stopper 19
Fountain 12, 13, *14*, 19, 20, 21, *27*, *28*
Durant, Sam 98
La Plus Belle Sculpture 98, *109*
Dürer, Albrecht 55
Durham, Jimmie 24
No one will be harmed. This is only a test 24, *51*

Enlightenment 56

Figaro, Le 96, *113*
film 23, 59
Foster, Hal 18
The Return of the Real 13
found objects 21
Freud, Sigmund 21

Gathering of the Tribes, A (New York gallery) 56
Genet, Jean 24
Gober, Robert 13, 19
A Pair of Basinless Sinks 19, *33*
Slides of a Changing Painting 19–20, *20*
Unfolding Door 55, *67*
Untitled [1991] 19, 20, *31*
Untitled [2000] *32*
Goldin, Nan 23
Graeser, Camille 56
Graham, Dan 98
grisaille collages 96

Hamilton, Richard 95
Hammons, David 13, 24
Blue Angels (Penises) 24, *38*
Flight Fantasy 56, *57*, *62–3*, *64–5*
Untitled [1974] *35*
Untitled [1975] *37*
Untitled (Hair Piece) 24, *36*
Hatoum, Mona 82–3
Corps étranger 83
Current Disturbance 14, 82, 83–4, *86–7*
The Light at the End 83, *83*
Recollection 83
Roadworks 83

Herrera, Arturo 95, 98
La Moto 114
Napule 114
Pedropar 115
Potsdam 115
Highmore, Ben 95
Hirst, Damien 59
Untitled (Collage 2) 59, *72*
Hockney, David 95
Hodges, Jim 24
Untitled (Everything So Alive Lively Living) 24, *39*

Indiana, Robert 95
installation 14, 23, *47*, *57*, 59, 82, 83–4, *84*, *86–7*, *88–9*, *91*, 99, *100*
Isaia, Despina: *Untitled* 24, *44–5*

J.L. Mott Iron Works 20
Jonas, Joan 98
Judd, Donald 55

Kandinsky, Wassily 95
Kawara, On 96
Kelley, Mike 13
Transplant 60, *74–5*
Kessanlis, Nikos 59
Gestures 59
Untitled (Gesture) 59, *73*
Kippenberger, Martin
I Am Too Political 96, *107*
Pop Art Calendar 95–6, *106*
Klein, Yves 59
Kracauer, Siegfried 94
Krauss, Rosalind 55
Kuri, Gabriel 98–9
Quick Standards 98, *117*

Le Corbusier 84
Levine, Sherrie 18, 20–21
Body Mask 21, *30*
Fountain (Buddha): 5 20, 21, *29*, *133*
LeWitt, Sol 56
Lichtenstein, Roy 95–6
Loos, Adolf *Ornament and Crime* 56
Lucas, Sarah *Bunny Gets Snookered #10* 23, *49*

Malevich, Kasimir 54
Mapplethorpe, Robert
Louise Bourgeois 21, *22*
Marshall, Richard 55
Mehretu, Julie 60
Untitled [66 x 101.6 cm] *79*
Untitled [71.1 x 101.6 cm] *78*
Minimalism 18, 55, 83
Modernism, Modernists 12, 21, 56, 59, 60, 95, 98
Mondrian, Piet 54
Morris, Robert 98

Nauman, Bruce 98
Double Steel Cage Piece 83, 84, *84*
Neuenschwander, Rivane 99
Contingent 99, *118–9*
new technologies 95, 96
Newkirk, Kori 56
Virgil 56, *69*
Newman, Barnett 54–5
Noland, Cady 95
Cowboy Eating, with Holes and Scarf in Crotch Hole 95, *105*
Objectification Process 95, *104*
Nouveau Réalisme (New Realism) 59

Orozco, Gabriel 94, 99
Empty Club 99, *100*
Moon Tree 99, *116*

painting 55, 60, 96, 98
Panopticon 84
Papastergiadis, Nikos 94
Partegàs, Ester 98
It's an Individual Experience (We the People Series) 98, *103*
performance 23, 24, 59, 82–3, *83*
photo-conceptual work 95
Picasso, Pablo 13, 54
Pistoletto, Michelangelo 98
Pollock, Jackson 13, 54–5
Pop art 95
Price, Seth
Untitled (Whispering, Feeding) 96, *108*
Prince, Richard 12

Ranard, John
NYC-35-95-David Hammons 57
rationalism 56
ready-mades 12, 13, *14*, 19, 20, 21, 24, *27*, *28*, 60, *73*, 94, 98, 99
Renaissance 55
Restany, Pierre 59
Romanticism 24
Roth, Dieter 56
Grafik mit Kakao 70
Large Landscape (Grosse Landschaft) 56, *71*
Small Landscape (Kleine Landschaft) 56, *70*
Rothko, Mark 54–5
Russian Constructivism 60

Schwitters, Kurt 59
sculpture 20, 21, 23, 24, 59, 82, 83
Sélavy, Rrose (Duchamp's female alter ego) 19
slide-projection 19-20
Smith, Kiki 13
Shitbody 23
Untitled 23, *46*
Smith, Tony 23
Smithson, Robert 98
Stieglitz, Alfred: *Fountain, photograph of sculpture by Marcel Duchamp* 12, *14*
Subkoff, Daniel 60
All Her Clothes Are Swept Aside by Her Face 60, *68*
Suprematism 54
Surrealism, Surrealists 18, 21, 23, 83, 95

Thek, Paul 21
Untitled (Meat Cable) 21, *42*
Tomkins, Calvin 21
Toroni, Niele 56
Trockel, Rosemarie 59
Avalanche 59, *77*
Something Of Tomorrow 59–60, *76*

Venice Biennale (1993) 99
video *47*, 55, 59, 82, 96, *118–9*

Walker, Kelley
Untitled 96, *97*, *113*
Warhol, Andy 13
Weiner, Lawrence 13
Williams, Sue 21, 23
Busy With Calm Background 41
Creamy Floral 41
Family Room 40
Wojnarowicz, David 23

Zurich Group 56

Acknowledgements

Thank you

The Whitechapel Gallery is grateful to the contributors who have made *Keeping it Real: An Exhibition in Four Acts* and its accompanying publication possible, in particular Mr and Mrs D. Daskalopoulos for their generosity in allowing the Whitechapel Gallery to exhibit their remarkable collection.

In addition we would like to thank François Chantala, Thomas Dane, Calum Sutton, Dimitris Paleocrassas and Ioanna Vryzaki for their invaluable input in the organisation of the exhibition and its publication.

We remain indebted to the artists whose work is exhibited in the programme, and the individuals and institutions who have consented to the reproduction of their work in this book:

Marina Abramović
Lynda Benglis
John Bock
Louise Bourgeois
Paul Chan
Marcel Duchamp
Sam Durant
Jimmie Durham
Robert Gober
David Hammons
Mona Hatoum
Arturo Herrera
Damien Hirst
Jim Hodges
Despina Isaia
Mike Kelley
Nikos Kessanlis
Martin Kippenberger
Sherrie Levine
Gabriel Kuri
Sarah Lucas
Julie Mehretu
Rivane Neuenschwander
Kori Newkirk
Cady Noland
Gabriel Orozco
Ester Partegàs
Seth Price
Dieter Roth
Kiki Smith
Daniel Subkoff
Paul Thek
Rosemarie Trockel
Kelley Walker
Sue Williams

The Whitechapel Gallery would also like to gratefully acknowledge the research assistance of Elizabeth Eames, Emma Enderby and Didem Yazici.

Supporters:

The Gallery thanks its supporters, whose generosity enables the realisation of its pioneering programme, in particular Hiscox, whose sponsorship of the Whitechapel Gallery's presentation of great collections underlines its commitment to promoting and protecting the very best in modern and contemporary art.

HISCOX

Whitechapel Project Major Donors
Arts Council England
Brian Boylan
City Bridge Trust
Cityside Regeneration
Dimitris Daskalopoulos
The Clore Duffield Foundation
English Heritage
Maryam & Edward Eisler
European Regional Development Fund
The Foyle Foundation
The Garfield Weston Foundation
Andrew & Antje Geczy
The Glass-House Trust
Richard & Janeen Haythornthwaite
Heritage Lottery Fund
Peter & Maria Kellner
Jack Kirkland
Brian & Lesley Knox
The Kresge Foundation
Leaside Regeneration
London Development Agency
David Matthews
The Mercers' Company
Keir McGuinness
Outset Contemporary Art Fund
Catherine & Franck Petitgas
Robert Taylor & Michael Kallenbach
Tishman Speyer Properties
Stavros Niarchos Foundation
Tower Hamlets
Dasha Shenkman
Bina & Philippe von Stauffenberg
Anita & Poju Zabludowicz
Nina & Michael Zilkha

Whitechapel Gallery Director's Circle
Fares & Tania Fares
Catherine & Franck Petitgas and those that wish to remain anonymous

Whitechapel Gallery Exhibition Patrons
Cranford Collection, London
Carolyn Dailey
Sarah & Louis Elson
Peter & Maria Kellner
Pascale Revert & Peter Wheeler
Renee & Mark Rockefeller
Maria & Malek Sukkar and those that wish to remain anonymous

Whitechapel Gallery Patrons
Charlotte & Alan Artus
Nasser Azam
John Ballington
Ariane Braillard & Francesco Cincotta
Hugo Brown
Sadie Coles HQ
Swantje Conrad
Alastair Cookson & Vita Zaman
Donall Curtin
DunnettCraven Ltd
Stephanie Dudzinski
Milovan Farronato
Nicoletta Fiorucci
Eric & Louise Franck
Alan & Joanna Gemes
David & Susan Gilbert
Gavin Graham
Louise Hallett
Cliff Ireton – Kingston Smith W1
Amrita Jhaveri
Matt & Kate Jones
David Keltie
Lisson Gallery
Victor & Anne Lewis

Keir McGuinness
Warren & Victoria Miro
Mary Moore
Dominic Morris & Sarah Kargan
Mummery + Schnelle
Angela Nikolakopoulou
Simon Oldfield Contemporary Art
Maureen Paley
Dominic Palfreyman
Ketan Patel
The Porter Foundation
Tim Rich
Judith Ritchie
Alex Sainsbury & Elinor Jansz
Kaveh & Cora Sheibani
Peter & Flora Soros
Bina & Philippe von Stauffenberg
Hugh & Catherine Stevenson
Cynthia Taylor
Helen Thorpe, The Helen Randag Charitable Foundation
Christoph & Marion Trestler
Emily Tsingou & Henry Bond
Kevin Walters
Cathy Wills
Iwan & Manuela Wirth
Withers LLP
Richard Wolff
Anita & Poju Zabludowicz and those that wish to remain anonymous

The American Friends of the Whitechapel Gallery
Bill & Alla Broeksmit
The Nightingale Code Foundation
Jolana & Petri Vainio
Marjorie G Walker
Audrey Wallrock
Cecilia Wong and those that wish to remain anonymous

Whitechapel Gallery Associates
Anne Berthoud
John & Tina Chandris
Carole & Neville Conrad
Crane Kalman Gallery
Philippa Found
Nicholas Fraser
Albert & Lyn Fuss
David Gill
Richard & Judith Greer
Elizabeth & Reade Griffith
Karen Groos
Mark & Sophia Lewisohn
George & Angie Loudon
Kate MacGarry
Carol Manheim, Biblion
Janet Martin
Penny Mason & Richard Sykes
James & Viviane Mayor
Wiebke Morgan & Nicholas Morgan
Lord & Lady Myners
John Newbigin
Chandrakant Patel
The Piccadilly Gallery
Lauren Prakke
Paul & Charlotte Pritchard
Alice Rawsthorn
Jon Ridgeway
Fozia Rizvi
David Ryder
Cherrill & Ian Scheer
Stuart Shave, Modern Art
Henrietta Shields
Liam & Jackie Strong and those that wish to remain anonymous

The Whitechapel Gallery is grateful for the on-going support of Members

Supported by ARTS COUNCIL ENGLAND

TOWER HAMLETS

Colophon

This catalogue has been published on occasion of:

Keeping it Real: An exhibition in four acts from the D. Daskalopoulos Collection

Whitechapel Gallery, London

9 June 2010 – 22 May 2011

Curated by
Achim Borchardt-Hume,
Chief Curator
Organised by
Shamita Sharmacharja,
Exhibitions Organiser

Publication design:
Rose, London
www.rosedesign.co.uk

Production and printing:
Push, London
www.push-print.com

Whitechapel Gallery is the imprint of Whitechapel Gallery Ventures Limited

A catalogue record for this book is available from the British Library.

First published by

Whitechapel Gallery
77–82 Whitechapel High Street
London E1 7QX
United Kingdom
Tel. +44 (0)20 7522 7888
Fax. +44 (0)20 7377 1685
info@whitechapelgallery.org
www.whitechapelgallery.org

To order (UK and Europe)
call +44 (0) 20 7522 7888 or
MailOrder@whitechapelgallery.org

Distributed to the book trade
(UK and Europe) by Central Books
www.centralbooks.com

ISBN: 978-0-85488-181-9

The Whitechapel Gallery is grateful to its generous supporters who are listed fully in the acknowledgements

Cover image:
Sherrie Levine
Fountain (Buddha): 5 (1996)
Cast bronze
42.5 x 40 x 30 cm

Whitechapel Gallery